I0333785

www.ingramcontent.com/pod-product-compliance
Lightning Source LLC
Chambersburg PA
CBHW051559010526
44118CB00023B/2751

Ajmal Al Qawaa'id

Student's Name: _____

Class / Year: _____

Teacher: _____

School / Madrasah: _____

CONTENTS

Ajmal Al Qawaa'id		Instructions for students	04
		Introduction to Ajmal Al Qawaa'id	06
		Pronunciation Diagram	08
Grade 01:	Lesson 01:	Alphabets	18
Grade 02:	Lesson 02:	Letters in Different Forms	28
Grade 03:	Lesson 03:	Fat-hah	40
	Lesson 04:	Kasrah	42
	Lesson 05:	Dhammah	44
Grade 04:	Lesson 06:	Fat-ha-tayn	50
	Lesson 07:	Kasra-tayn	52
	Lesson 08:	Dhamma-tayn	54
Grade 05:	Lesson 09:	Fat-hah followed by Alif	60
	Lesson 10:	Madd Fat-hah	64
	Lesson 11:	Madd Kasrah	66
	Lesson 12:	Madd Dhammah	68
Grade 06:	Lesson 13:	Sukoon	74
Grade 07:	Lesson 14:	Fat-hah followed by Waw Saakin	80
	Lesson 15:	Dhammah followed by Waw Saakin	82
Grade 08:	Lesson 16:	Fat-hah followed by Ya Saakin	88
	Lesson 17:	Kasrah followed by Ya Saakin	90
Grade 09:	Lesson 18:	Shaddah	98
Grade 10:	Lesson 19:	Silent letters in words	108
	Lesson 20:	Silent Alif	110
	Lesson 21:	Special words	112
	Lesson 22:	Words with a jerking sound	114

Completed on   /   /

Grade 11:	Lesson 23:	Small Madd	118
	Lesson 24:	Big Madd	120
	Lesson 25:	Big Madd followed by a Shaddah	122
Grade 12:	Lesson 26:	Qalqalah	126
	Lesson 27:	Ghunnah	128
	Lesson 28:	Izhaar	130
Grade 13:	Lesson 29:	Rule of the letter Ra	134
	Lesson 30:	Rule of the word Allaah	136
Grade 14:	Lesson 31:	Idghaam and silent letters	140
	Lesson 32:	Idghaam	142
Grade 15:	Lesson 33:	Ikhfaa	148
	Lesson 34:	Ikhfaa Meem	150
	Lesson 35:	Iqlaab	152
	Lesson 36:	Noon Qutni	154
Grade 16:	Lesson 37:	Stopping on round Ta (Ta Marbootah)	158
	Lesson 38:	Stopping on Fat-ha-tayn	160
	Lesson 39:	Waqf (Stopping)	162
	Lesson 40:	Waqf (Stopping) on three words	164
	Lesson 41:	Saktah	166
Grade 17:	Lesson 42:	Advance stopping and Sajdah	170
	Lesson 43:	Huroof Al-Muqatta'aat	172
	Lesson 44:	Complete Verse Fluency	174
Grade 18:	Lesson 45:	Last 10 Surahs	180

Comments

INSTRUCTIONS FOR STUDENTS

 Do Wudhu before reading your Qaa'idah.

 Come early and refresh your lesson before reading to your teacher.

 Sit with respect infront of your teacher.

 Whenever beginning the session read Ta'awwudh (A'oodhu Billaahe Minash Shaytaanir Rajeem). Always start reading your lesson with Tasmiyah (Bismillaahir Rahmaanir Raheem).

 Point at the word you're reading with your right index finger.

 Avoid only reading your lesson once or twice. Keep practicing until you're called to read to the teacher so you progress to the next lesson.

Always listen to the teacher attentively whilst they are explaining the lesson.

 If you do not understand the lesson ask the teacher to explain it until you understand.

 Always put your hand up if you want to ask the teacher anything.

 Never disrespect the teacher by speaking back to them.

 Avoid speaking unnecessarily to your friends during your learning time.

 Ensure that you are wearing the correct uniform and that you have all your learning resources with you.

 Remind yourself of all the beautiful rewards of learning the Qur'aan.

INTRODUCTION TO AJMAL AL QAWAA'ID

This book has been designed to help make reading the Qur'aan easy. It is important to understand why certain tools have been included and how to make use of them.

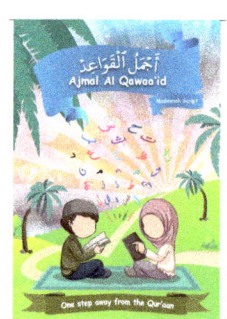

The Grades
This book has been divided into 18 grades. Gradually preparing the student by building solid foundations before progressing to the advance rules.
Each grade is a foundation for the following grade. It is important that each level is mastered before progressing to the next.

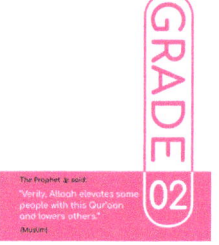

The Overview
This is a teacher/parent section where each lesson will be explained in detail. Teachers will know what needs to be taught and how. Parents will know exactly what their child's targets are and how to support their learning at home.

The Arabic page
This is the most important page in the book and needs to be learnt properly. Each page has its own learning objective and targets hence requires lots of practice.

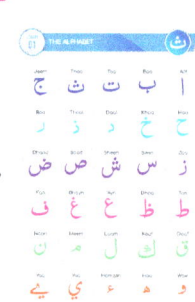

The Star reward system and completed on section

At the bottom of the Arabic page there will be 'three stars' that will be used by teachers to monitor progress regularly. Once the lesson is completed the date will be written on the 'completed on' section by the teacher.

 = Requires more practice
= Completed with assistance but needs some practice
= Independently completed and ready to move on

Step by step

This section will explain the Arabic page step by step in detail. Looking at the Arabic page and reading the relevant part of this section together will make the learning and understanding easier.

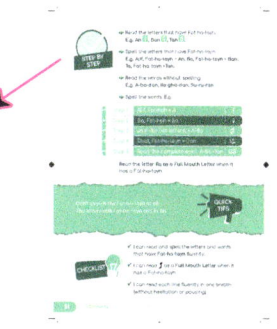

Quick tips

This section will include valuble guidance from experienced teachers.

Checklist

This self-assessment section needs to be completed by the student before progressing onto the next lesson.

Comments

Parents and teachers can comment as and when required.

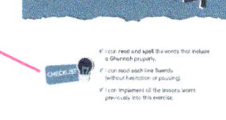

PRONUNCIATION DIAGRAM

Every letter is pronounced from a specific part of the mouth and throat. Take a look at each letters origin point and familiarise yourself with them.

خ غ Sound produced from the Top of the Throat

ح ع Sound produced from the Middle of Throat

ء ه Sound produced from the Bottom of the Throat

ق – **Back of the Tongue** to touch the roof of the Mouth.

ك – **Middle of the tongue but closer to the back**
to touch the roof of the mouth.

ج ش ي – **Middle of the tongue but closer to the front** to touch the roof of the mouth.

ض – **Side of the tongue** to touch the top back teeth.

ل – **Tip of the tongue (flat)** to touch the gums of the top front teeth.

ن – **Tip of the tongue (flat)** to touch the gums of the top front teeth.

ر – **Tip and edge of the tongue** to touch the gums of the top teeth.

ط د ت – **Tip of the tongue** to touch the root of the top front 2 teeth.

ث ذ ظ - **Tip of the tongue** to touch the tip of the top front 2 teeth.

س ز ص - **Tip of the tongue** to touch the edge of the bottom 2 teeth whilst slightly touching the top 2 teeth as well.

     Completed on   /   /

ف – **The inner part of the lower lip** to touch the tip of the top two teeth.

ب – **The inner part of both lips** to touch each other.

م – **The Outer part of both lips** to touch each other.

Notes

GRADE 01

The Prophet ﷺ said:

"The best amongst you is he who learns the Qur'aan and teaches it to others."

(Bukhaari)

OVERVIEW

LESSON 01 > THE ALPHABET

- Each letter should be **pronounced correctly.**
- Students must be able to identify and recognise each letter correctly i.e. with its dots, similarities and differences in shapes etc.
- Students must memorise the entire alphabet with its **correct pronunciation.**
- Students must memorise the entire alphabet by reading the letters and **mentioning how many dots each letter has** i.e. Alif has no dots, Baa has one dot below, Taa has two dots above etc.
- To build fluency the teacher may point out a random letter and ask the student to identify it.

EXERCISE 01 — Full Mouth Letters

- The student must be able to **identify** and **read** the **full mouth letters** correctly with complete confidence. The full mouth letters are highlighted in blue.

EXERCISE 02 — Mixed Alphabets

- The student must be able to read the **mixed alphabets** with **complete confidence** and with **fluency.**

LESSON 01 — THE ALPHABET

Alif	Baa	Taa	Thaa	Jeem
أ	ب	ت	ث	ج

Haa	Khaa	Daal	Thaal	Raa
ح	خ	د	ذ	ر

Zaa	Seen	Sheen	Saad	Dhaad
ز	س	ش	ص	ض

Taa	Dhaa	'Ayn	Ghayn	Faa
ط	ظ	ع	غ	ف

Qaaf	Kaaf	Laam	Meem	Noon
ق	ك	ل	م	ن

Waw	Haa	Hamzah	Yaa	Yaa
و	ه	ء	ي	ى

Completed on   /   /

18

- Identify each letter with its correct pronunciation.
- Read the **entire alphabet** fluently from memory.
- Recognise the differences in the shapes of the letters.

Recognise, learn and memorise the alphabet by reading each letter.

E.g. **Alif,** has no dots
      Baa, has one dot at the bottom
      Taa, has two dots on top

This will aid your letter recognition.

The best way to memorise the letters is to have interesting links to them.

E.g. The smiley face letter = ت
      The amazing letter = و
      The snake letter = س
      (make your own)

- I can read the entire **Arabic alphabet** fluently.
- I can **pronounce** all the letters correctly.
- I can **recognise** the differences in the **shapes of the letters** and the number of dots they have from memory fluently.

EXERCISE 01 — FULL MOUTH LETTERS

أ	ب	ت	ث	ج
ح	خ	د	ذ	ر
ز	س	ش	ص	ض
ط	ظ	ع	غ	ف
ق	ك	ل	م	ن
و	ه	ء	ي	ىے

Completed on   /   /

- Identify each **full mouth letter** with its correct pronunciation.
- Read the entire **full mouth letters** fluently from memory.
- Recognise the **differences in the shapes** of the letters.

Read the **full mouth letters** as if your mouth is full of food or full of air.

- I can recognise and pronounce all the **full mouth letters** properly.
- I can read the entire alphabet aloud **from memory.**
- I can implement all the lessons learnt previously into this exercise.

EXERCISE 02 — MIXED ALPHABETS

ز	ذ	ط	ج	ب	أ	ت	ح
ش	ث	ض	ق	ع	غ	ظ	خ
د	ء	ك	ي	م	و	ه	ف
ب	ذ	ق	س	ل	ص	ر	ن
أ	ف	ك	د	غ	ث	ح	ظ
ش	ع	ء	ي	و	ج	م	ض
ن	ج	ذ	ع	ص	ي	ل	ط
ظ	ق	ف	ح	ث	غ	ر	ت
ض	ي	ع	ء	ش	م	و	ك

STEP BY STEP

- ▸ Read out all the letters **fluent**ly with their correct pronunciation.
- ▸ Read one **entire line** without hesitation or pausing.
- ▸ Recognise the **differences in the shapes** of the letters.

QUICK TIPS

Read in random order, pointing at random letters and read them as quickly as possible.

Keep reading the letters in groups of 3 until your speed increases, then do the next group until you have read the whole line.

CHECKLIST

- ◉ I can read all the letters in **mixed form** without referring back to the previous pages.
- ◉ I can read an **entire line without pausing**.
- ◉ I can implement all previous lessons learnt into this exercise.

Notes

GRADE 02

The Prophet ﷺ said:

"Verily, Allaah elevates some people with this Qur'aan and lowers others."

(Muslim)

OVERVIEW

LETTERS IN DIFFERENT FORMS

- This lesson shows how each letter is written at the **beginning, middle and end of each word**.
- Ask the student to identify the similarities between the **joint form letters** and the large letters (dots, shape etc).

EXERCISE 01   Special letters and Single form letters

- The **Special Letters** do not join with **the letters that come after it**, examples of these letters are given in words.
- The student should build fluency in identifying **single letters** before moving on to the **two letter words**, then **three letter words** etc.
- Advanced students may attempt to identify all the letters.

EXERCISE 02   Dual and Plural letters

- Further explain how the letters are joined to make words.
- The gaps between the letters in the first two lines are there to help distinguish each letter.
- The student should not hesitate or pause when reading the words.
- The student may refer to previous lessons as guidance particularly with identifying the **Special Letters**.

EXERCISE 03   Extension

- The students should be able to identify and pronounce each letter correctly.
- Each line must be read without any hesitation or pausing. The student should be reminded to attempt reading the word quickly and accurately.
- This will help build fluency and consistency in their recitation.
- Students must be **confident** in recognising all the **different forms of letters** by this stage before progressing on to the next grade.

LESSON 02
LETTERS IN DIFFERENT FORMS

أ	ب	ت	ث	ج
أأأ	ببب	تتتة	ثثث	ججج

ح	خ	د	ذ	ر
ححح	خخخ	ددد	ذذذ	ررر

ز	س	ش	ص	ض
ززز	سسس	ششش	صصص	ضضض

ط	ظ	ع	غ	ف
ططط	ظظظ	ععع	غغغ	ففف

ق	ك	ل	م	ن
ققق	ككك	للل	ممم	ننن

و	ه	ء	ي
ووو	ههه	ئئئ	ييي

- ▸ Recognise the **letters in different forms**.
- ▸ Read each line **without pausing**.
- ▸ Identify the similarities between the **Single Form Letters** and the Joint Form Letters.

- ▸ Identify the similarities between the Single Form Letters and the Joint Form Letters using the dots method.
- ▸ Remember! When the letter **Yaa** ي is written at the end of a word, it may not have any dots.

- ⓒ I can identifiy all the **letters in different forms**.
- ⓒ I can read the letters in **different forms** without hesitation or pausing.
- ⓒ I can implement all the lessons learnt previously into this exercise.

EXERCISE 01 — SPECIAL LETTERS

أ	د	ذ	ر	ز	و
↓	↓	↓	↓	↓	↓
أحد	دكا	ذهب	رفع	زعم	وجد

أحد   دكا   ذهب   رفع   زعم   وجد

SINGLE FORM LETTERS

ش	ظ	غ	م	خ	ك	ج	ت
ا	ض	ب	ئ	و	س	ف	ذ
ح	ع	ز	ث	ر	ن	ي	ص
ق	ه	د	ط	ك	ه‍	ف	ئ
ل	ض	ذ	ق	ب	ع	ظ	ت

Completed on   /   /

- ▶ Recognise the **Special Letters** and understand their roles
- ▶ Read the **Single Form Letters** in standalone form
- ▶ Read **two letter** words fluently and accurately

Remember, **Alif** for Allaah, **Daal, Thaal, Ra, Za** come together and finally **Waw.** Wow! for learning the 'Special Letters'.

- ○ I can recognise all the **Special Letters**.
- ○ I can read all the **Joint Form Letters** clearly and fluently.
- ○ I can implement all the lessons learnt previously into this exercise.

Comments

EXERCISE 02 — TWO LETTER WORDS — طه

ثذ	غق	فة	حم	يس	طه
طل	نض	مغ	لد	خع	طس
يي	نى	لى	ثى	تى	بى

يي	نى	لى	ثى	تى	بى

THREE LETTER WORDS

نبى	تمت	سنن	لكن	حزب	يحب
تجد	نخل	عجل	يحى	لوح	تحت
خزى	جبل	لحق	عوج	لبث	فتح
حجج	هاد	جمع	داع	مهد	بخل

Completed on / /

- ▸ Read the letters fluently when written together to form words. E.g. 'Taa', 'Haa'.
- ▸ Read **two letter words** fluently and accurately.
- ▸ Recognise the letters 'Baa', 'Taa', 'Thaa', 'Laam', 'Noon' and 'Yaa', when written together with a 'Yaa'.

يي نى لى ثى تى بى

- ▸ Put a line through the join and remember that the top letter comes first and it's dots would be on it or below it. The top letter would either be a Baa, Taa, Thaa, Laam, Noon or Yaa depending on where the dots are.
- ▸ The letter below will be a Yaa. Yaa is written without its dots when it comes at the end of the word.
- ▸ Practice one line at a time as **quickly as possible**, keep repeating it until your speed increases. Then move onto the next one.

- ✓ I can recognise **all the letters** when written as a word.
- ✓ I can read the letters when written as a word **fluently in one breath.**
- ✓ I can implement all previous lessons learnt into this exercise.

EXERCISE 03 — EXTENSION

بر	تر	ثر	نر	ير
	ج	ح	خ	

نحيا	ونخل	نحلة	نجنى	يجعل
نجيا	ونخل	نحلة	نجنى	يجعل

يخفف	بحبل	بخلوا	تحزنا	بخبر
يخفف	بحبل	بخلوا	تحزنا	بخبر

يجير	تجرى	يخلف	تخفى	نخيل
يجير	تجرى	يخلف	تخفى	نخيل

يحيين	ثجاجا	يختص	أنجينا	يجتبى
يحيين	ثجاجا	يختص	أنجينا	يجتبى

- ▸ Read out all the letters fluently with their correct pronunciation.
- ▸ Read one entire line **without taking a breath** (without hesitation or pausing).
- ▸ Recognise the letters 'Ba', 'Jeem', 'Kha', 'Noon', when written together.

بِخُبْرٍ تَخْزُنَا ثَجَاجًا نَجْنِى يُخَفِّفُ

- ▸ Put a line through the join and remember that the top letter comes first and it's dots would be on it or below it.
- ▸ The top letter would either be a Baa, Taa, Thaa, Noon or Yaa depending on the dots.
- ▸ The letter below will either be a Jeem, Ha or Kha.

- ⓘ I can read all the letters in **mixed form** without referring back to the previous pages.
- ⓘ I can **read an entire line** without pausing.
- ⓘ I can implement all previous lessons learnt into this exercise.

Notes

GRADE 03

The Prophet ﷺ said:

"Read the Qur'aan, for it will come as an intercessor for its reciters on the Day of Resurrection."

(Muslim)

OVERVIEW

The Fat-hah gives an **A** sound and **should not be stretched**.
- ▸ The letter **Ra** will be pronounced as a **Full Mouth Letter** when it has a Fat-hah above it: رَ
- ▸ The letter **Ya** ى does not always come with dots, so familiarise yourself with the shape.

Harakaat = Symbols (such as Fat-hah, Kasrah, Dhammah etc).

The Kasrah gives an **E** sound and **should not be stretched**.
- ▸ The letter **Ra** will be pronounced as an **Empty Mouth Letter** when it has a Kasrah beneath it: رِ
- ▸ The letter **Ya** ى does not always come with dots, so familiarise yourself with the shape.

The Dhammah gives an **U** sound and **should not be stretched**.
- ▸ The letter **Ra** will be pronounced as an **Full Mouth Letter** when it has a Dhammah above it: رُ
- ▸ The letter **Ya** ى does not always come with dots, so familiarise yourself with the shape.

* Extension = More practice before progressing further.

LESSON 03 — FAT-HAH

أَ بَ تَ ثَ جَ حَ خَ دَ ذَ رَ

زَ سَ شَ صَ ضَ طَ ظَ عَ غَ فَ

قَ كَ لَ مَ نَ وَ هَ ءَ يَ

EXERCISE

سَبَق   كَتَب   حَذَر   هَلَك   فَصَل

بَسَر   وَهَن   طَبَع   عَبَس   ذَرَأ

وَقَع   فَعَل   سَقَر   شَرَح   وَزَر

شَجَر   رَفَث   خَلَق   وَهَب   حَجَر

فَخَرَج   وَظَهَر   كَشَف   دَخَل   مَعَك

STEP BY STEP

- ▸ Read the letters that have Fat-hah.
  E.g. "A" أ, "Ba" بَ, "Ta" كَ.

- ▸ Spell the letters that have a Fat-hah.
  E.g. Alif, Fat-hah = A. Ba, Fat-hah = Ba.
  Ta, Fat-hah = Ta.

- ▸ Read the words.
  E.g. Fa-Sa-La, Ha-La-Ka, Ha-Tha-Ra.

- ▸ Spell the words that have Fat-hah. E.g.

Step 1	Fa, Fat-hah = Fa	فَ
Step 2	Saad, Fat-hah = Sa	صَ
Step 3	Join the two, Fa-Sa	فَصَ
Step 4	Laam, Fat-hah = La	لَ
Step 5	Read the entire word, Fa-Sa-La	فَصَلَ

Read the letter **Ra** as a **Full Mouth Letter** when it has a Fat-hah.

QUICK TIPS

- ▸ **Don't stretch** the Fat-hah at all.
- ▸ The letters with Fat-hah all end with the sound **A**.

CHECKLIST

- ⓒ I can read and spell the **letters and words** that have a **Fat-hah** fluently.
- ⓒ I can read the letter **Ra** as a **Full Mouth Letter** when it has a Fat-hah.
- ⓒ I can read each line fluently in one breath (without hesitation or pausing).

Comments

LESSON 04 — KASRAH

إِ بِ تِ ثِ جِ حِ خِ دِ ذِ رِ

زِ سِ شِ صِ ضِ طِ ظِ عِ غِ فِ

قِ كِ لِ مِ نِ وِ هِ ءِ يِ

EXERCISE

كَبِر حَفِظ تَرِن شِيَة أَمِنَ

إِبِل عَلِمَ إِرَمَ فَلِمَ أَبَتِ

بَلَدِ مَلِكِ وَسِعَ حَطِبِ كَرِهَ

وَعَمِلَ وَوَرِثَ وَقَعَتِ يَئِسَ شِيِع

لِخَزَنَتِ بِيَدِكَ أَفَأَمِنَ بِعِصَمٍ وَخَسِرَ

- Read the letters that have Kasrah.
  E.g. E إِ, Be بِ, Te تِ.

- Spell the letters that have Kasrah.
  E.g. Alif, Kasrah = E. Ba, Kasrah = Be.
  Ta, Kasrah = Te.

- Read the words.
  E.g. A-Me-Na, She-Ya-Ta, Ta-Ra-Ne.

- Spell the words that have Kasrah. E.g.

Step 1	Alif, Fat-hah = A	أَ
Step 2	Meem, Kasrah = Me	مِ
Step 3	Join the two, A-Me	أَمِ
Step 4	Noon, Fat-hah = Na	نَ
Step 5	Read the entire word, A-Me-Na	أَمِنَ

Read the letter **Ra as an Empty Mouth Letter** when it has a Kasrah.

 QUICK TIPS

- **Don't stretch** the Fat-hah and Kasrah at all.
- The letters with Kasrah all end with the sound E.

- I can read and spell the **letters and words** that have a **Kasrah** fluently.
- I can read each line **fluently in one breath** (without any hesitation or pausing).
- I can implement all the lessons learnt previously into this exercise.

Comments

LESSON 05 — DHAMMAH

أُ بُ تُ ثُ جُ حُ خُ دُ ذُ رُ

زُ سُ شُ صُ ضُ طُ ظُ عُ غُ فُ

قُ كُ لُ مُ نُ وُ هُ ءُ يُ

EXERCISE

لُعِنَ   يَعِدُ   هُدِى   أَجِدُ   نُفِخَ

حُبِّكِ   أَعِظُ   حُشِرَ   تَجِدُ   يَرِثُ

سُبُلَ   ذُكِرَ   سُقِطَ   أُخَرُ   قُضِى

وُضِعَ   كَبُرَ   نُقِرَ   بُغِىَ   عُفِىَ

يَعِدُ   أُذُنِ   كُبِتَ   خَبُثَ   أُفِكَ

STEP BY STEP

- ▶ Read the letters that have a Dhammah.
  E.g. U اُ , Bu بُ , Tu تُ .

- ▶ Spell the letters that have Dhammah.
  E.g. Alif, Dhammah = U. Ba, Dhammah = Bu.
  Ta, Dhammah = Tu.

- ▶ Read the words.
  E.g. Lu-'E-Na, Ya-'E-Du, Hu-De-Ya.

- ▶ Spell the words that have Dhammah. E.g.

Step 1	Laam, Dhammah = Lu	لُ
Step 2	'Ayn, Kasrah = 'E	عِ
Step 3	Join the two, Lu-'E	لُعِ
Step 4	Noon, Fat-hah = Na	نَ
Step 5	Read the entire word. Lu-'E-Na	لُعِنَ

Read the letter **Ra as a Full Mouth Letter** when it has a Dhammah.

QUICK TIPS

- ▶ **Don't stretch** the **Fat-hah, Kasrah** and **Dhammah** at all.
- ▶ As soon as you point at a word you should be able to read it without thinking for too long. The letters with Dhammah all end with the sound **U**.

CHECKLIST

- ✓ I can read and spell the **letters and words** that have a **Dhammah** fluently.
- ✓ I can read the letter **Ra as a Full Mouth Letter** when it has a **Dhammah**.
- ✓ I can read each line **fluently in one breath** (without any hesitation or pausing).

LESSON 03-05 — EXTENSION

يَكُ   قَمَرَ   ذَكَرَ   وُجِدَ   رَفَعَ

عَدَلَ   ظَلَمَ   كُتِبَ   مَثَلُ   نَظَرَ

زَعَمَ   سَرَقَ   صَدَقَ   كَسَبَ   تَزِرُ

قُتِلَ   عَهِدَ   وَجَدَ   يَرِثُ   تَرَكَ

شَهِدَ   رَدِفَ   كُفِرَ   جَرَمَ   زُبُرِ

قُدِرَ   ضَرَبَ   بَعَثَ   وَنُذُرِ   ذَهَبَ

صُحُفِ   لَنُبِذَ   فَنَذَرُ   كَلِمَتُ   عَمَلُكَ

فَجُمِعَ   وَتَصِفُ   خَلَقَكَ   عَضُدَكَ   فَبَصَرُكَ

- ▸ Read out all the letters fluently with their correct pronunciation.
- ▸ Read an entire line without taking a breath.

- ▸ Read in a random order, pointing at random letters and reading them as quickly as possible.
- ▸ Harakaat = Symbols (such as Fat-hah, Kasrah, Dhammah etc).

- ✓ I can read all the words that have **Fat-hah, Kasrah and Dhammah** fluently.
- ✓ I can read an entire line without pausing.
- ✓ I can implement all previous lessons learnt into this exercise.

GRADE 04

The Prophet ﷺ said:
"Whoever reads the Qur'aan and memorises it, Allaah will admit him to Paradise and allow him to intercede for ten of his family members who all deserved to enter Hell."

(Ibn Majah)

OVERVIEW

Fat-ha-tayn is a Fat-hah sound with an **N sound** at the end and should not be stretched.
(Fat-ha-tayn always comes at the end of a word, and mostly with an Alif).
- The letter Ra will be pronounced as a Full Mouth Letter when it has a Fat-ha-tayn above it: رً
- The letter Ya ي does not always come with dots, so familiarise yourself with the shape.

Kasra-tayn is a Kasrah sound with an **N sound** at the end and should not be stretched. (Kasra-tayn always comes at the end of a word).
- The letter Ra will be pronounced as a Empty Mouth Letter when it has a Kasra-tayn beneath it: رٍ
- The letter Ya ي does not always come with dots, so familiarise yourself with the shape.

Dhamma-tayn is a Dhammah sound with an **N sound** at the end and should not be stretched. (Dhamma-tayn always comes at the end of a word).
- The letter Ra will be pronounced as a Full Mouth Letter when it has a Dhamma-tayn above it: رٌ
- The letter Ya ي does not always come with dots, so familiarise yourself with the shape.
- **Tanween = Fat-ha-tayn, Kasra-tayn and Dhamma-tayn.**

Extension = More practice before progressing further.

LESSON 06: FAT-HA-TAYN

أً بًا تًا ثًا جًا حًا خًا دًا ذًا رًا

زًا سًا شًا صًا ضًا طًا ظًا عًا غًا فًا

قًا كًا لًا مًا نًا وًا هًا ئًا يًا

EXERCISE

أَبَدًا رَغَدًا سُرُرًا حَزَنًا ذُلُلًا

عَضُدًا سَكَرًا عِوَجًا مَلِكًا سَعَةً

طَرَفًا صَعِقًا شُهُبًا سَكَنًا قَدَرًا

شَطَطًا لُبَدًا خَطَئًا نُزُلًا وَزُلَفًا

أَمَنَةً حَسَنَةً بَقَرَةً وَحَفَدَةً صَدَقَةً

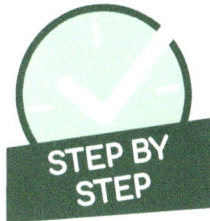

STEP BY STEP

• Read the letters that have Fat-ha-tayn.
  E.g. An ً, Ban ً, Tan ً.

• Spell the letters that have Fat-ha-tayn.
  E.g. Alif, Fat-ha-tayn = An. Ba, Fat-ha-tayn = Ban. Ta, Fat-ha-tayn = Tan.

• Read the words without spelling.
  E.g. A-ba-dan, Ra-gha-dan, Su-ru-ran.

• Spell the words. E.g.

Step 1	Alif, Fat-hah = A	أَ
Step 2	Ba, Fat-hah = Ba	بَ
Step 3	Join the two letters, = A-Ba	أَبَ
Step 4	Daal, Fat-ha-tayn = Dan	دًا
Step 5	Read the complete word, A-Ba-Dan	أَبَدًا

Read the letter **Ra** as a **Full Mouth Letter** when it has a Fat-ha-tayn.

QUICK TIPS

• Don't stretch the Fat-ha-tayn at all.
• The letters with Fat-ha-tayn end in An.

CHECKLIST

✓ I can read and spell the letters and words that have **Fat-ha-tayn** fluently.

✓ I can read ﺭ as a **Full Mouth Letter** when it has a Fat-ha-tayn.

✓ I can read each line fluently in one breath (without hesitation or pausing).

LESSON 07 — KASRA-TAYN

إِ بِ تِ ثِ جِ حِ خِ دِ ذِ رِ

زِ سِ شِ صِ ضِ طِ ظِ عِ غِ فِ

قِ كِ لِ مِ نِ وِ هِ ءِ يِ

EXERCISE

لِسَبَإٍ   حَمَإٍ   خَبَرٍ   فِئَةٍ   أُمَمٍ

سُرُرٍ   شَجَرٍ   سَحَرٍ   سَنَتٍ   بَرَدٍ

وَدُسُرٍ   وَسُعُرٍ   مَطَرٍ   سُوَرٍ   فُرُشٍ

ثَمَرَةٍ   رَقَبَةٍ   هُمَزَةٍ   سَفَرَةٍ   بِسَحَرٍ

بِصَدَقَةٍ   بِسَخَطٍ   بِغَضَبٍ   لُمَزَةٍ   بَرَرَةٍ

- ▸ Read the letters that have Kasra-tayn.
  E.g. In ٍ, Bin ٍبٍ, Tin ٍتٍ.

- ▸ Spell the letters that have Kasra-tayn.
  E.g. Alif, Kasra-tayn = In. Ba, Kasra-tayn = Bin.
  Ta, Kasra-tayn = Tin.

- ▸ Read the words without spelling.
  E.g. U-ma-min, Fe-a-tin, Kha-ba-rin.

- ▸ Spell the words. E.g.

Step 1	Alif, Dhammah = U	أُ
Step 2	Meem, Fat-hah = Ma	مَ
Step 3	Join the two letters, U-Ma	أُمَ
Step 4	Meem Kasra-tayn = Min	مٍ
Step 5	Read the complete word = U-Ma-Min	أُمَمٍ

- •▸ Don't stretch the Fat-ha-tayn and Kasra-tayn at all.
- •▸ The letters with Kasra-tayn end in 'In'.

Note: When Jeem, Haa, khaa, 'Ayn and Ghayn come at the end of a word the Kasra-tayn will be written in their stomachs not at the bottom.

- ✓ I can read and spell the letters and words which have **Kasra-tayn** fluently.
- ✓ I can read each line **fluently in one breath** (without hesitation or pausing).
- ✓ I can implement all the lessons learnt previously into this exercise.

LESSON 08 — DHAMMA-TAYN

أٌ بٌ تٌ ثٌ جٌ حٌ خٌ دٌ ذٌ رٌ

زٌ سٌ شٌ صٌ ضٌ طٌ ظٌ عٌ غٌ فٌ

قٌ كٌ لٌ مٌ نٌ وٌ هٌ ءٌ يٌ

EXERCISE

أَخٌ   قَتَرَةٌ   مَلَأٌ   حُمُرٌ   أَشِرٌ

سَكَنٌ   قِطَعٌ   وَلَدٌ   فِئَةٌ   سُنَنٌ

غُرَفٌ   كُتُبٌ   نَصَبٌ   لَفَرِحٌ   نَجَسٌ

وَبِيعٌ   خُشُبٌ   سِنَةٌ   حُرُمٌ   جُدَدٌ

كَلِمَةٌ   فَنَظِرَةٌ   وَجِلَةٌ   فَرَجُلٌ   فَعَجَبٌ

- Read the letters that have Dhamma-tayn.
  E.g. Oon اً, Boon بٌ, Toon تٌ.

- Spell the letters that have Dhamma-tayn.
  E.g. Alif, Dhamma-tayn = Oon. Ba, Dhamma-tayn = Boon. Ta, Dhamma-tayn = Toon.

- Read the words without spelling.
  E.g. A-khoon, Qa-ta-roon, Ma-la-oon.

- Spell the words. E.g.

Step 1	Alif, Fat-hah = A	اَ
Step 2	Kha, Dhamma-tayn = Khoon	خٌ
Step 3	Read the complete word, A-Khoon	اَخٌ

Read the letter **Ra as a Full Mouth Letter** when it has a Dhamma-tayn.

QUICK TIPS

- Don't stretch the Fat-ha-tayn, Kasra-tayn and Dhamma-tayn at all.

- The letters with Dhamma-tayn end in Oon.

CHECKLIST

- I can read and spell the letters and words that have **Dhamma-tayn** fluently.

- I can read رٌ as a **Full Mouth Letter** when it has a Dhamma-tayn.

- I can read each line fluently in one breath (without hesitation or pausing).

مَثَلًا	بَشَرٌ	ذَهَبًا	نَكِدًا	أَحَدٍ
بِدَمٍ	كُفُوًا	أَسِفًا	لَبَنًا	حَرِجٍ
مَلَكٌ	رُسُلٌ	عَمَلٌ	مَرَضٌ	بَلَدٍ
نَهَرٍ	قَسَمٌ	لَعِبًا	رَهَقًا	هُزُوًا
رَصَدًا	عَلَقٍ	أُذُنٌ	لَعِبٌ	أَجَلُ
أُكُلٍ	سُرُرٌ	شَجَرٌ	ثَمَنًا	ظَمَأُ
رَشَدًا	سَفَرٍ	قَدَمٌ	كُتُبٌ	غَضَبٍ
غَبَرَةٌ	عَلَقَةٍ	كَبِدٍ	حَكَمًا	سُقُفًا
دَرَجَةٌ	حَسَنَةٌ	بَقَرَةٌ	شَجَرَةٌ	قَتَرَةٌ

- ▸ Read and spell all the words **fluently** with their correct pronunciation.
- ▸ Read an **entire line** without taking a breath or pausing.

- ▸ Read in a random order, pointing at random words, reading them as quickly as possible.
- ▸ Practice one word at a time until you have read a whole line. Then try to say it all in one go.

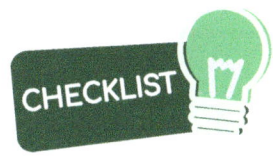

- I can **read and spell** all the words **quickly**.
- I can read an **entire line** without pausing.
- I can implement all the lessons learnt previously into this exercise.

GRADE 05

The Prophet ﷺ said:

"The one who was devoted to the Qur'an will be told on the Day of Resurrection: 'Recite and ascend (in ranks) as you used to recite when you were in the world. Your rank will be at the last Ayah you recite."

(Abu Dawood and Tirmidhi)

OVERVIEW

  FAT-HAH FOLLOWED BY AN ALIF

- Fat-hah followed by an Alif is a stretched Fat-hah.
- A letter with a Fat-hah followed by an empty Alif without a Harakah (symbol) above it will be stretched to **double the stretch of a Fat-hah** (1 second).

 MADD FAT-HAH

- Madd Fat-hah is a stretched Fat-hah.
- A letter with a Madd Fat-hah will be stretched to **double the stretch of a Fat-hah** (1 second).

 MADD KASRAH

- Madd Kasrah is a stretched Kasrah.
- A letter with a Madd Kasrah will be stretched to **double the stretch of a Kasrah** (1 second).

 MADD DHAMMAH

- Madd Dhammah is a stretched Dhammah.
- A letter with a Madd Dhammah will be stretched to **double the stretch of a Dhammah** (1 second).

* Extension = More practice before progressing further.

LESSON 09: FAT-HAH FOLLOWED BY AN ALIF

بَا

بَا تَا ثَا جَا حَا خَا دَا ذَا رَا زَا

سَا شَا صَا ضَا طَا ظَا عَا غَا فَا قَا

كَا لَا مَا نَا وَا هَا ئَا يَا

EXERCISE

ذَاتَ خَافَ كَانَ تَابَ نَارًا

هَادٍ عَابِدٌ نَبَاتَ حَافِظُ ثُبَاتٍ

جُنَاحَ كَاتِبٌ مَالِكُ غَاسِقٍ ثَوَابًا

جَاعِلٌ دَابِرَ صَوَابًا أَفَاقَ خَالِدًا

وَلَعَلَا مُطَاعٍ أَصَابَ يَخَافُ كَوَاعِبَ

- Read the letters that have an Alif.
  E.g. Baa بَا, Taa تَا, Thaa ثَا.

- Spell the letters that have an Alif.
  E.g. Ba, Alif Fat-hah = Baa. Ta, Alif Fat-hah = Taa. Tha, Alif, Fat-hah = Thaa.

- Read the words without spelling.
  E.g. Thaa-ta, Khaa-fa, Kaa-na.

- Spell the words. E.g.

Step 1	Thaal, Alif Fat-hah = Thaa	ذَا
Step 2	Ta, Fat-hah = Ta	تَ
Step 3	Read the entire word, Thaa-Ta	ذَاتَ

Read the letter **Ra as a Full Mouth Letter** when it has a Fat-hah and an Alif.

QUICK TIPS

- If an empty Alif comes after a Fat-hah letter, it will be stretched twice the length of a Fat-hah.

- As soon as you point at a word you should be able to read it straight away.

- I can read and spell words which have **Fat-hah and Alif fluently**.

- I can read رَا as a **Full Mouth Letter** when it comes with a Fat-hah and Alif.

- I can read each line fluently in one breath (without hesitation or pausing).

LESSON 09 — SINGLE AND DUAL WORDS

بَا

زَالَتَا	أَسَاوِرَ	سَأَلَهَا	زَاهِقٌ	فَوَاكِهَ
دَافِقٍ	مَوَاخِرَ	هَامِدَةً	تَظَاهَرَا	بِوَلَدِهَا
عَلَانِيَةً	فَتَطَاوَلَ	سُرَادِقُهَا	مُتَرَاكِبًا	مُتَشَابِهٍ

وَلَاحَامٍ	فَلَاتُمَارِ	فَلَاجُنَاحَ
مَاوَعَدَنَا	نَارًا أَحَاطَ	لَا طَاقَةَلَنَا
كَانَ فَاسِقًا	كَانَ مِزَاجُهَا	أَصَابَهَا وَابِلٌ
سَحَابًاثِقَالًا	تِجَارَةً حَاضِرَةً	غِلَاظٌ شِدَادٌ
وَعَدَسِهَاوَبَصَلِهَا	عَالِيَهَاسَافِلَهَا	طَعَامِكَ وَشَرَابِكَ
وَلَا تَزِرُ وَازِرَةٌ	بَابًاذَاعَذَابٍ	لِبَاسَهُمَا لِيُرِيَهُمَا

STEP BY STEP

- Read and spell the single and dual words that have **Fat-hah** followed by an Alif.
- Read the dual and plural words **quickly and properly** without pausing.
- Read each line without stopping after the words.

QUICK TIPS

Look at all the symbols carefully, remember not to stretch the Fat-hah, Kasrah and Dhammah letters.

CHECKLIST

- I can **read and spell** the letters and words **quickly and fluently**.
- I can read each line **fluently in one breath** (without hesitation or pausing).
- I can implement all the lessons learnt previously into this exercise.

LESSON 10 — MADD FAT-HAH

١-

أَ بَ تَ ثَ جَ حَ خَ دَ ذَ رَ

زَ سَ شَ صَ ضَ طَ ظَ عَ غَ فَ

قَ كَ لَ مَ نَ وَ هَ ءَ يَ

EXERCISE

إِلَهَ   ءَايَتِ   ءَاتَهُ   تُرَبًا   غُلَمًا

تَشَبَهَ   ظَهِرًا   عِظَمًا   تَزَوَرُ   ضِعَفًا

سُلَلَةٍ   غِشَوَةً   شَمِخَةٍ   قَصِرَةٌ   وَاحِدَةً

يَصَلِحُ   كَلِمَتٍ   كَشِفَتُ   حَسَرَتٍ   بِفَحِشَةٍ

خَلَتِكَ   رِسَلَتِ   قَنِتَتٌ   حَفِظَتُ   مُتَجَوِرَتٌ

- Read the letters that have a Madd Fat-hah. E.g. Aa آ, Baa بَ, Taa تَ.

- Spell the letters. E.g. Alif, Madd Fat-hah = Aa. Ba, Madd Fat-hah = Baa. Ta, Madd-Fat-hah = Taa.

- Read the words without spelling. E.g. E-laa-ha, Aa-yaa-te, Ra-aa-hu.

- Spell the words. E.g.

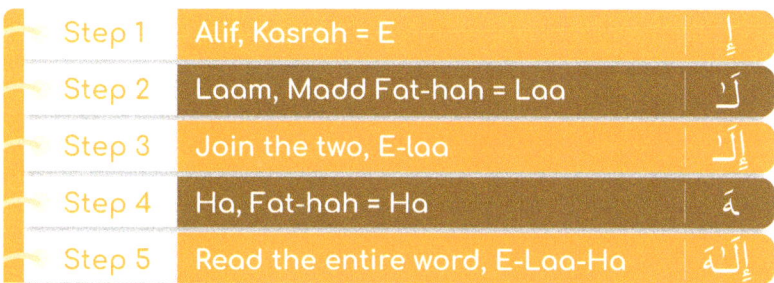

Step 1	Alif, Kasrah = E	اِ
Step 2	Laam, Madd Fat-hah = Laa	لَا
Step 3	Join the two, E-laa	اِلَا
Step 4	Ha, Fat-hah = Ha	هَ
Step 5	Read the entire word, E-Laa-Ha	اِلَهَ

Read the letter **Ra as a Full Mouth Letter** when it has a Madd Fat-hah.

QUICK TIPS

- Stretch the Madd Fat-hah twice the length of a Fat-hah (1 second).

- As soon as you point at a word you should be able to read it straight away.

CHECKLIST

- I can **read and spell** the words which have **Madd Fat-hah** fluently.

- I can read رَا as a **Full Mouth Letter** when it comes with a Madd Fat-hah.

- I can read each line **fluently in one breath** (without hesitation or pausing).

LESSON 11: MADD KASRAH

إِ بِ تِ ثِ جِ حِ خِ دِ ذِ رِ

زِ سِ شِ صِ ضِ طِ ظِ عِ غِ فِ

قِ كِ لِ مِ نِ وِ هِ ءِ يِ

EXERCISE

بِهِ   هَٰذِهِ   وَلَدِهِ   عَقِبِهِ   بِيَدِهِ

ءَايَٰتِهِ   عَمَلِهِ   قِبَلِهِ   ثَمَرِهِ   عُنُقِهِ

أَجَلِهِ   عُمُرِهِ   وَالِدِهِ   بَصَرِهِ   وَرُسُلِهِ

عِبَادِهِ   جِهَادِهِ   طَعَامِهِ   رِسَٰلَتِهِ   نِعَاجِهِ

تِلَاوَتِهِ   شَاكِلَتِهِ   بِشِمَالِهِ   مَوَاضِعِهِ   نَثَا بِجَانِبِهِ

STEP BY STEP

- Read the letters that have a Madd Kasrah.
  E.g. Ee اِ , Bee بِ , Tee تِ .

- Spell the letters that have a Madd Kasrah.
  E.g. Alif, Madd Kasrah = Ee. Ba, Madd Kasrah = Bee. Ta Madd kasrah = Tee.

- Read the words without spelling.
  E.g. Be-hee, Haa-the-hee, Wa-la-de-hee.

- Spell the words. E.g.

Step 1	Ba, Kasrah = Be	بِ
Step 2	Ha, Madd Kasrah = Hee	هِي
Step 3	Read the entire word, Be-Hee	بِهِي

QUICK TIPS

- Stretch the Madd Kasrah twice the length of a Kasrah (1 second).

- As soon as you point at a word you should be able to read it straight away.

CHECKLIST

- I can **read and spell** the words which have **Madd Kasrah** fluently.

- I can read each line **fluently in one breath** (without hesitation or pausing).

- I can implement all the lessons learnt previously into this exercise.

LESSON 12: MADD DHAMMAH

وو

أُو بُو تُو ثُو جُو حُو خُو دُو ذُو رُو

زُو سُو شُو صُو ضُو طُو ظُو عُو غُو فُو

قُو كُو لُو مُو نُو وُو هُو ءُو يُو

EXERCISE

فَعَلَهُو	سَمِعَهُو	مَلَأَهُو	أَمَرَهُو	رُسُلَهُو
خِتْمُهُو	أَجَلَهُو	قَدَرُهُو	وَثَاقَهُو	ظِلَلَهُو
فَتَرَكَهُو	فِصَلُهُو	بَيَانَهُو	وَزَادَهُو	خُمْسَهُو
بَرَكَّتُهُو	أَمَانَتَهُو	حِسَابَهُو	فَأَمَاتَهُو	صَلَاتَهُو
وَبَاطِنَهُو	يُحَاوِرُهُو	فَأَصَابَهُو	مَفَاتِحَهُو	فَيُضْعِفَهُو

Completed on / /

STEP BY STEP

- ▸ Read the letters that have a Madd Dhammah.
  E.g. Oo أُ, Boo بُ, Too تُ.

- ▸ Spell the letters that have Madd Dhammah.
  E.g. Alif, Madd Fat-hah = Oo. Ba, Madd Dhammah = Boo. Ta, Madd Dhammah = Too.

- ▸ Spell the words. E.g.

Step		
Step 1	Fa, Fat-hah = Fa	فَ
Step 2	'Ayn, Fat-hah = 'A	عَ
Step 3	Join the letters, Fa-'A	فَعَ
Step 4	Laam, Fat-hah = La	لَ
Step 5	Join the letters, Fa-'A-la	فَعَلَ
Step 6	Ha, Madd Dhammah = Hoo	هُو
Step 7	Read the entire word, Fa-'A-la-hoo	فَعَلَهُو

QUICK TIPS

- ▸ Stretch the Madd Dhammah twice the length of a Dhammah (1 second).

- ▸ As soon as you point at a word you should be able to read it straight away.

CHECKLIST

- ✓ I can **read and spell** the words which have **Madd Dhammah** fluently.

- ✓ I can read each line **fluently in one breath** (without hesitation or pausing).

- ✓ I can implement all the lessons learnt previously into this exercise.

EXERCISE 09-12 EXTENSION

فَئَامَنَ لَهُۥ	إِلَٰهُهُۥ وَهَوَىٰهُ	ءَالَ دَاوُۥدَ
لَهُۥ وَلَهُۥ	مَعَهُۥ أَخَاهُ	إِلَٰهًا ءَاخَرَ
لَاعِوَجَ لَهُۥ	هَٰذِهِۦ نَاقَةٌ	ذَٰلِكَ لَأٓيَةً

وَمَا كَانَ لَهُۥ	تَابَ وَءَامَنَ	ذَٰلِكَ قَوَامًا
هَٰذَا بِئَالِهَتِنَا	هَٰذَا ٱلسَّحِرُ	ثَالِثُ ثَلَٰثَةٍ
خَلَقَهُۥ وَبَدَأَ	فَصِيَامُ ثَلَٰثَةٍ	كَانَ بِعِبَادِهِۦ

هَٰذَا مَا وَعَدَنَا	وَثُلَٰثَ وَرُبَٰعَ	لَجَعَلَهُۥ سَاكِنًا
إِذَا جَعَلَهُۥ نَارًا	مَالُهُۥ وَوَلَدُهُۥ	وَكَانَ لَهُۥ ثَمَرٌ

فَإِذَا أَصَابَ بِهِۦ عَمَلِهِۦ فَرَءَاهُ حَسَنًا لَقِيَا غُلَٰمًا فَقَتَلَهُۥ

- Read and spell the dual and plural words that include all previous Harakaat on them fluently:
  - Fat-hah, Kasrah and Dhammah
  - Fat-ha-tayn, Kasra-tayn and Dhamma-tayn
  - Fat-hah letters followed by an empty Alif
  - Madd Fat-hah, Madd Kasrah and Madd Dhammah
- Read the **dual and plural words quickly** and properly without pausing.
- Read each line **without stopping** after the words.

- Only stretch the letter that has a Fat-hah and Alif, Madd Fat-hah, Madd Kasrah and Madd Dhammah.
- The letter Ra will read with an empty mouth when it comes with a Kasrah or Madd Kasrah, otherwise it will always be read with a full mouth.

Note: The Hamzah will be written in the middle of Laam and Alif لَأْ , this will mean you will stretch the Hamzah because of the Alif.

- I can **read and spell** the letters and words fluently.
- I can read each line **fluently in one breath** (without hesitation or pausing).
- I can implement all the lessons learnt previously into this exercise.

Comments

GRADE 06

The Prophet ﷺ said:

"Read the Qur'aan, for it will come as an intercessor for its reciters on the Day of Resurrection."

(Muslim)

OVERVIEW

LESSON 13 > **SUKOON**

- A letter with a **Sukoon** أَنْ on it indicates that the sound of the letter before it will be joining onto it.
  The letter that has a Sukoon on it is known as a **Saakin** letter.

EXERCISE 01   SUKOON IN SINGLE AND DUAL WORDS

- Students should be able to **identify** and **read** all the words that have a **Sukoon** or **multiple Sukoon's** in them.

- **Alif with a small Saad** on top ٱ is silent and will be ignored.

LESSON 13: SUKOON

مِنْ	بَلْ	أَمْ	إِذْ	أَنْ
دَعْ	عِدْ	سَلْ	عَنْ	قُلْ
كُلْ	قَدْ	ذُقْ	هَبْ	خُذْ
يَتْبُ	مِثْلَ	لَحْمَ	فَصْرُ	أَتَتْ
رِزْقٍ	إِثْمٌ	أَمْرٍ	سِحْرٌ	كُرْهًا
نَقْعًا	طَلْعٌ	بَعْضَ	نَخْلٍ	نَحْسٍ
بَلْدَةً	أَلْقَى	كَلْمَحِ	تَنْزِعُ	فَضْلًا
تَرَكْنَا	طَعْمُهُ	شَطْأَهُ	أَقْبَلَ	غَمْرَةٍ
قَسْمَنَا	تَبْصِرَةً	نِعْمَةً	تَحْبَطْ	أَظْلَمَ

• Read the words that have a Sukoon.
E.g. An , Am .

• Spell the words. E.g.

| Step 1 | Alif, Noon, Fat-hah = An | أَنْ |

When you see a letter with a Sukoon, join it to the letter before.

QUICK TIPS

✓ I can **read and spell** the Saakin letters and words.

✓ I can read each line **fluently in one breath** (without hesitation or pausing).

✓ I can implement all the lessons learnt previously into this exercise.

EXERCISE 01: SUKOON IN SINGLE AND DUAL WORDS

أَضْحَكَ	قُرْبَانًا	مَغْفِرَةً	أَنْزَلَ	بَعْضًا
مُنْتَشِرٌ	أَثَابَهُمْ	مُسْتَطَرٌ	مُقْتَدِرٍ	مُحْتَظِرٍ
أَنْتُمْ	مُنْتَصِرٌ	صَرْصَرًا	لِتَسْتَوُوا	تَنْتَصِرَانِ

بَعْضُهُمْ	يُجْرِكُمْ	فَعَلْتُمْ	إِفْكُهُمْ	يَبْخَلْ
أَعْمَالَهُمْ	تُصِبْكُمْ	رِزْقُكُمْ	ظَنَنْتُمْ	أَعْتَدْنَا
أَبْصَارُهُمْ	أَرْسَلْنَاكَ	أَرْحَامَكُمْ	فِتْنَتَكُمْ	أَنْفُسِكُمْ

وَنَحْنُ أَقْرَبُ	مِنْهُمْ بَطْشًا	بَعْدَ ظُلْمِهِ
تَوَارَتْ بِالْحِجَابِ	أَسْتَجِبْ لَكُمْ	سَمْعِهِ وَقَلْبِهِ

- ▸ Read and spell the words that include two Saakin letters in one word fluently.
- ▸ Read and spell the **double words** confidently and fluently. E.g.

Step 1	Ba, 'Ayn, Fat-hah = Ba'	بَعْ
Step 2	Dhaad, Fat-ha-tayn = Dhan	ضًا
Step 3	Read the entire word, Ba'-Dhan	بَعْضًا

QUICK TIPS

Remember, it is a quick join!

Alif with small Saad آ = Silent

- ✓ I can **read and spell** the **dual Saakin** letters and words.
- ✓ I can read each line **fluently in one breath** (without hesitation or pausing).
- ✓ I can implement all the lessons learnt previously into this exercise.

GRADE 07

The Prophet ﷺ said:

"Read the Qur'aan regularly. By the One in Whose Hand Muhammad's soul is, it escapes from memory faster than a camel does from its tying ropes."

(Muslim)

OVERVIEW

LESSON 14 > **FAT-HAH FOLLOWED BY A 'WAW' SAAKIN**

- When a **Waw Saakin** (Waw with a Sukoon) comes after a letter with a Fat-hah, the Fat-hah letter will be **read without a stretch**.

*Note: When a Waw Saakin comes after a Fat-hah at the end of a word with an Alif and a circle above it ا , this **Alif will be silent**.*

LESSON 15 > **DHAMMAH FOLLOWED BY A 'WAW'**

- When a **Waw without a Sukoon** comes after a letter with Dhammah, the Dhammah letter will be **read with a stretch of 1 second**.
- The stretch will be similar to Madd Dhammah.

*Note: When a Waw without a Sukoon comes after a Dhammah at the end of a word with an Alif and a circle above it ا , this **Alif will be silent**.*

EXERCISE 01   DUAL WORDS

The student must be confident in reading the bigger words that include **Fat-hah/Dhammah followed by a Waw**. These words will give them the practice they need so when they move on they know where to apply the stretch and where not to.

*Note: When a **Waw is missing its Sukoon** this means that the letter before it will be read with a stretch.*

LESSON 14: FAT-HAH FOLLOWED BY A 'WAW' SAAKIN

أَوْ

أَوْ بَوْ تَوْ ثَوْ جَوْ حَوْ خَوْ دَوْ ذَوْ رَوْ

زَوْ سَوْ شَوْ صَوْ ضَوْ طَوْ ظَوْ عَوْ غَوْ فَوْ

قَوْ كَوْ لَوْ مَوْ نَوْ وَوْ هَوْ ءَوْ يَوْ

EXERCISE

يَرَوْا	زَوْجًا	سَوْفَ	غَوْرًا	رَوْحُ
عَصَوْا	خَلَوْا	سَوْطَ	صَوْمًا	لَوْحٍ
كَوْكَبًا	مَوْتِهَا	تَوْبَةً	حَوْلَهُ	عَفَوْنَا
يَنْهَوْنَ	مَوْعِدُهُ	بِعَوْرَةٍ	قَوْمُكَ	غَدَوْتَ
مُسْتَوْدَعٌ	أَوْلَـٰدُهُم	يُجْزَوْنَ	مَوْلَـٰهُم	تَنْسَوْنَ

- Read the small words without spelling.
  E.g. Aw أَوْ, Baw بَوْ, Taw تَوْ.

- Spell the small words that include a Fat-hah followed by a Waw Saakin.
  E.g. Alif, Waw, Fat-hah = Aw. Ba, Waw, Fat-hah = Baw. Ta, Waw, Fat-hah = Taw.

- Read the words. E.g. Rawhoon, Ghawran, Sawfa.

- Spell the words. E.g.

Step 1	Ra, Waw, Fat-hah = Raw	رَوْ
Step 2	Ha, Dhamma-tayn = Hoon	حٌ
Step 3	Read the entire word, Raw-Hoon	رَوْحٌ

QUICK TIPS

When Fat-hah is joining onto Waw Saakin أَوْ, don't stretch the sound of the Fat-hah letter.

E.g. Fat-hah followed by Waw Saakin = Aw.

CHECKLIST

- I can **read and spell** the **Fat-hah followed by a Waw Saakin**.
- I can read each line **fluently in one breath** (without hesitation or pausing).
- I can implement all the lessons learnt previously into this exercise.

Comments

LESSON 15: DHAMMAH FOLLOWED BY A 'WAW'

أُو

رُو ذُو دُو خُو حُو جُو ثُو تُو بُو أُو

فُو غُو عُو ظُو طُو ضُو صُو شُو سُو زُو

يُو ءُو هُو وُو نُو مُو لُو كُو قُو

EXERCISE

تَكُونُواْ   أَوْقَدُواْ   فَعَلُواْ   أَوْفُواْ   قَالُواْ

يَخَافُواْ   نَتْلُوهَا   مَوْزُونٍ   مَوْفُورًا   سَارِعُواْ

مَغْلُولَةٌ   يَعْرِفُونَهُۥ   يُرْجَعُونَ   خَسِرُواْ   تَصْبِرُواْ

وَٱخْتَلَفُواْ   يَفْقَهُوهُ   وَٱعْتَصِمُواْ   تُرْحَمُونَ   يُخَٰدِعُونَ

تَلْبَسُونَهَا   تَهْتَدُونَ   فَيَنْقَلِبُواْ   يَعْتَدُونَ   مُتْرَفُوهَا

     Completed on   /   /

- Read the small words without spelling.
  E.g. Oo اُو, Boo بُو, Too تُو.

- Spell the small words that include a Dhammah followed by a Waw.
  E.g. Alif, Waw, Dhammah = Oo. Ba, Waw, Dhammah = Boo. Ta, Waw, Dhammah = Too.

- Read the words. E.g. Qaaloo, Awfoo, Fa'aloo.

- Spell the words. E.g.

Step 1	Qaaf, Alif, Fat-hah = Qaa	قَا
Step 2	Laam, Waw, Dhammah = Loo	لُوْ
Step 3	Read the whole word, Qaa-Loo	قَالُوْ

QUICK TIPS

When a Dhammah is joining onto a Waw اُو, stretch the sound of the Dhammah letter for around a second or so.
Alif with a round circle اْ = Silent
E.g. Dhammah followed by Waw Saakin = Oo.

CHECKLIST

- I can read and spell the **Dhammah followed by a Waw**.
- I can read each line **fluently in one breath** (without hesitation or pausing).
- I can implement all the lessons learnt previously into this exercise.

EXERCISE 01 — DUAL WORDS

يَقَوْمِ ٱذْكُرُواْ	وَلْيَقُولُواْ قَوْلًا	وَقَوْلِهِمْ قُلُوبُنَا
تَعَالَوْاْ قَاتِلُواْ	وَٱكْسُوهُمْ وَقُولُواْ	فَسَوْفَ تَعْلَمُونَ
وَرَفَعْنَا فَوْقَهُمْ	يُقَاتِلُواْ قَوْمَهُمْ	أَوْ تُخْفُوهُ أَوْ تَعْفُواْ
وَسَوْفَ تُسْئَلُونَ	أَوِ ٱلْخَوْفِ أَذَاعُواْ	هَاجَرُواْ وَأُخْرِجُواْ
وَلَا تَهِنُواْ وَلَا تَحْزَنُواْ	وَأَصْلَحُواْ وَٱعْتَصَمُواْ	وَقَعَدُواْ لَوْ أَطَاعُونَا
قَٰتَلُوكُمْ فَٱقْتُلُوهُمْ	أَوْسَطِ مَا تُطْعِمُونَ	وَرَسُولَهُ وَيَسْعَوْنَ
وَصَابِرُواْ وَرَابِطُواْ	نُشُوزًا أَوْ إِعْرَاضًا	ثَقِفْتُمُوهُمْ وَأَخْرِجُوهُمْ
جَمَعُواْ لَكُمْ فَٱخْشَوْهُمْ	فَلَا تَخْشَوْهُمْ وَٱخْشَوْنِ	ظُهُورِهِمْ وَٱشْتَرَوْاْ بِهِۦ

Completed on / /

STEP BY STEP

•▶ Spell the words. E.g.

Step		
Step 1	Ya, Madd, Fat-hah = Yaa	يَا
Step 2	Qaaf, Waw, Fat-hah = Qaw	قَوْ
Step 3	Join the two letters, Yaa-Qaw	يَقَوْ
Step 4	Meem, Thaal, Kasrah = Mith	مِ ذْ
Step 5	Join all previous, Yaa-Qaw-Mith	يَقَوْمِ ذْ
Step 6	Kaaf Dhammah = Ku	كُ
Step 7	Join all previous, Yaa-Qaw-Mith-Ku	يَقَوْمِ ذْكُ
Step 8	Ra, Waw, Dhammah = Roo	رُوْا
Step 9	Read the entire word, Yaa-Qaw-Mith-Ku-Roo	يَقَوْمِ ذْكُرُوْا

•▶ Fat-hah joining onto a Waw أَوْ = **No stretch**

•▶ Dhammah joining onto a Waw أُوْ = **Stretch**

QUICK TIPS

CHECKLIST

✓ I can **read and spell** the words that have a **Waw Saakin** fluently.

✓ I can read each line **fluently in one breath** (without hesitation or pausing).

✓ I can implement all the lessons learnt previously into this exercise.

Comments

GRADE 08

The Prophet ﷺ said:

"Read the Qur'aan, for it will come as an intercessor for its reciters on the Day of Resurrection."

(Muslim)

OVERVIEW

LESSON 16 — **FAT-HAH FOLLOWED BY A 'YA' SAAKIN**

- When a **Ya Saakin** (Ya with a Sukoon) comes after a letter with a Fat-hah, the Fat-hah letter will be **read without a stretch**.

LESSON 17 — **KASRAH FOLLOWED BY A 'YA'**

- When a **Ya without a Sukoon** comes after a letter with a Kasrah, the Kasrah letter will be **read with a stretch of 1 second**.
- The stretch will be similar to Madd Kasrah.

EXERCISE 01 — DUAL AND PLURAL WORDS

The student must be confident in reading the bigger words that include **Fat-hah/Kasrah followed by a Ya**. These words will give them the practice they need so when they move on they know where to apply the stretch and where not to.

EXERCISE 02 — SHORT VERSE FLUENCY

The student will get a feel of the bigger words and sentences as they appear in the Qur'aan.
The teacher should take a mini test at this stage before progressing the child to the next grade. If the student is applying all the rules properly and reading fluently then they should move on otherwise should revise anything they may need polishing.
This will give them extra practice and boost their confidence.

Note: When a Ya or a Waw is missing its Sukoon this means that the letter before it will be read with a stretch.

LESSON 16: FAT-HAH FOLLOWED BY A 'YA' SAAKIN — أَيْ

أَيْ بَيْ تَيْ ثَيْ جَيْ حَيْ خَيْ دَيْ ذَيْ رَيْ

زَيْ سَيْ شَيْ صَيْ ضَيْ طَيْ ظَيْ عَيْ غَيْ فَيْ

قَيْ كَيْ لَيْ مَيْ نَيْ وَيْ هَيْ ئَيْ يَيْ

EXERCISE

بَيْتِهِ	رُوَيْدًا	رَأَيْتَ	طَيْرًا	مَيْتًا
أَبَوَيْهِ	قَضَيْنَا	صَيْحَةً	ذَوَاتَيْ	فَأَبَيْنَ
أَوْدَيْنِ	إِلَهَيْنِ	حَيْرَانَ	عَقِبَيْهِ	كَهَيْئَةِ
فَتَعَالَيْنَ	فَأَحْيَيْنَهُ	وَهَدَيْنَهُمْ	زَوْجَيْنِ	شَفَتَيْنِ
فَأَغْشَيْنَهُمْ	فَأَغْوَيْنَكُمْ	وَاجْتَبَيْنَهُمْ	لَهَدَيْنَهُمْ	بِالْوَالِدَيْنِ

- ▶ Read the small words without spelling.
  E.g. Ay أَيْ, Bay بَيْ, Tay تَيْ.

- ▶ Spell the small words that include a Fat-hah followed by a 'Ya' Saakin.
  E.g. Alif, Ya, Fat-hah = Ay. Ba, Ya, Fat-hah = Bay. Ta, Ya, Fat-hah = Tay.

- ▶ Read the words. E.g. Maytan, Tayran, Ra-'ayta.

- ▶ Spell the words. E.g.

Step 1	Meem, Ya, Fat-hah = May	مَيْ
Step 2	Ta, Fat-ha-tayn = Tan	تًا
Step 3	Read the whole word, May-Tan	مَيْتًا

When Fat-hah is joining onto a Ya Saakin أَيْ, don't stretch the sound of the Fat-hah letter.

E.g. Fat-hah followed by Ya Saakin = Ay.

- ◉ I can **read and spell** the **Fat-hah followed by a Ya Saakin**.
- ◉ I can read each line **fluently in one breath** (without hesitation or pausing).
- ◉ I can implement all the lessons learnt previously into this exercise.

LESSON 17: KASRAH FOLLOWED BY A 'YA'

إِى بِى تِى ثِى جِى حِى خِى دِى ذِى رِى

زِى سِى شِى صِى ضِى طِى ظِى عِى غِى فِى

قِى كِى لِى مِى نِى وِى هِى ئِى يِى

EXERCISE

بَنِينَ دِينًا أَثِيمًا سَلِيمٍ أَبْغِى

شِيعَتِهِۦ أَرُونِى أَقِيمُوا۟ لَيَبْغِى طَٰغِينَ

مُدْبِرِينَ يَٰلَيْتَنِى مُقْنِعِى تَبْدِيلًا سَيُصِيبُ

يُطِيقُونَهُۥ تُصَحِبْنِى مُهْطِعِينَ مِسْكِينًا غَرَابِيبُ

سَيَجْزِيهِمْ لِتَسْتَبِينَ سَرَابِيلُهُمْ بِمَبْعُوثِينَ مُعْرِضِينَ

STEP BY STEP

- ▸ Read the small words without spelling.
  E.g. Ee إِي, Bee بِي, Tee تِي.

- ▸ Spell the small words that include a Kasrah followed by a 'Ya'. E.g. Alif, Ya, Kasrah = Ee. Ba, Ya, Kasrah = Bee. Ta, Ya, Kasrah = Tee.

- ▸ Read the words.
  E.g. Ab-ghee, Salee-min, Athee-man.

- ▸ Spell the words. E.g.

Step 1	Alif, Ba, Fat-hah = Ab	أَبْ
Step 2	Ghayn, Ya, Kasrah = Ghee	غِي
Step 3	Read the whole word, Ab-Ghee	أَبْغِي

QUICK TIPS

When a Kasrah is joining onto a Ya إِي, stretch the sound of the Kasrah letter for around a second or so.

E.g. Kasrah followed by Ya = Eee.

CHECKLIST

- ✓ I can **read and spell** the Kasrah followed by a Ya.

- ✓ I can read each line **fluently in one breath** (without hesitation or pausing).

- ✓ I can implement all the lessons learnt previously into this exercise.

Comments

EXERCISE 01 — DUAL AND PLURAL WORDS

وَأَكِيدُ كَيْدًا	إِبْرَاهِيمَ خَلِيلًا	خَيْرًا كَثِيرًا
صَلَاتِي وَنُسُكِي	عَلَيْهِمْ شَهِيدًا	عَلَيْكَ عَظِيمًا
خَالِدِينَ فِيهَا	وَمُهَيْمِنًا عَلَيْهِ	إِلَيْهِمْ خَاشِعِينَ

عَلَيْكُمْ نِعْمَتِي	غَيْرَ مُسَافِحِينَ	رَأَيْتَ ٱلْمُنَافِقِينَ
غَيْرَ مَعْرُوشَاتٍ	فَلَمَسُوهُ بِأَيْدِيهِمْ	مَقَامِي وَتَذْكِيرِي
فَتَنْقَلِبُوا۟ خَاسِرِينَ	فَأَشْهِدُوا۟ عَلَيْهِمْ	بِوُجُوهِكُمْ وَأَيْدِيكُمْ

وَأُوذُوا۟ فِي سَبِيلِي	وَلَا يُظْلَمُونَ نَقِيرًا	وَٱرْزُقُوهُمْ فِيهَا
مُذَبْذَبِينَ بَيْنَ ذَٰلِكَ	أُجُورَكُمْ يَوْمَ ٱلْقِيَامَةِ	كَانَ عَلَيْكُمْ رَقِيبًا
وَٱتْلُ عَلَيْهِمْ نَبَأَ ٱبْنَيْ	نُمْلِي لَهُمْ لِيَزْدَادُوا۟	فَأَفُوزَ فَوْزًا عَظِيمًا

STEP BY STEP

•▶ Spell the words. E.g.

Step		
Step 1	Kha, Ya, Fat-hah = Khay	خَيْ
Step 2	Ra, Fat-ha-tayn = Ran	رًا
Step 3	Join the two letters, Khay-Ran	خَيْرًا
Step 4	Kaaf, Fat-hah = Ka	كَ
Step 5	Join all previous, Khay-Ran-Ka	خَيْرًاكَ
Step 6	Tha, Ya, Kasrah = Thee	ثِي
Step 7	Join all previous, Khay-Ran-Ka-Thee	خَيْرًاكَثِي
Step 8	Ra, Fat-ha-tayn = Ran	رًا
Step 9	Read the entire word, Khay-Ran-Ka-Thee-Ran	خَيْرًاكَثِيرًا

QUICK TIPS

- •▶ Fat-hah joining onto a Waw أَوْ , or Fat-hah joining a Ya أَيْ = No stretch.
- •▶ Dhammah joining onto a Waw أُو , or Kasrah joining onto a Ya إِي = Stretch

CHECKLIST

- ◉ I **can read and spell** the words that have a Ya Saakin fluently.
- ◉ I can read each line **fluently in one breath** (without hesitation or pausing).
- ◉ I can implement all the lessons learnt previously into this exercise.

EXERCISE 02 — SHORT VERSE FLUENCY

قَدْ أَنزَلْنَا عَلَيْكُمْ لِبَاسًا	وَجَدَ عِندَهَا رِزْقًا
وَخُلِقَ ٱلْإِنسَٰنُ ضَعِيفًا	أَن تَمِيلُوا۟ مَيْلًا عَظِيمًا
وَمَا جَعَلْنَٰكَ عَلَيْهِمْ حَفِيظًا	لِمَ تَقُولُونَ مَا لَا تَفْعَلُونَ
يُصْهَرُ بِهِۦ مَا فِى بُطُونِهِمْ	فَمَنْ أَبْصَرَ فَلِنَفْسِهِۦ
وَهُوَ أَعْلَمُ بِٱلْمُهْتَدِينَ	مَنْ أَرْسَلْنَا عَلَيْهِ حَاصِبًا

لِمَ تَعْبُدُ مَا لَا يَسْمَعُ وَلَا يُبْصِرُ وَلَا يُغْنِى عَنكَ شَيْـًٔا

فَمَنْ ءَامَنَ وَأَصْلَحَ فَلَا خَوْفٌ عَلَيْهِمْ وَلَا هُمْ يَحْزَنُونَ

لَئِنْ أُخْرِجُوا۟ لَا يَخْرُجُونَ مَعَهُمْ وَلَئِن قُوتِلُوا۟ لَا يَنصُرُونَهُمْ

- Read and spell the small sentences.
- Apply the **stretch on the correct letters**.
- Read an entire sentence without pausing or hesitation.

QUICK TIPS

If an empty Alif comes between two words وَخُلِقَ ٱلْإِنسَٰنُ it will be ignored.
Split the big words into smaller chunks, and read them efficiently before reading the whole word.

- I can **read and spell the sentences** correctly and fluently.
- I can read each **sentence in one breath** (without hesitation or pausing).
- I can implement all the lessons learnt previously into this exercise.

Comments

GRADE 09

The Prophet ﷺ said:
"Whoever recites a letter from the Book of Allaah, he will be credited with a good deed, and a good deed gets a ten-fold reward. I do not say that Alif-Laam-Meem is one letter, but Alif is a letter, Laam is a letter and Meem is a letter."

(Muslim)

OVERVIEW

LESSON 18 > **SHADDAH STRONG JOIN** ّ

The Shaddah ّ represents the merging of two letters, one with a Sukoon and the other with a Harakah: رَبَّ = بَ + رَبْ
Listen to the student carefully so that they are pronouncing the strong join properly.
The student should be confident and fluent in reading with spelling and without spelling.

Alif with a small Saad on top ٱ is silent and will be ignored.

EXERCISE 01   Double Shaddah words

The student must be confident in reading Shaddah letters properly when appearing in bigger words: وَٱلرُّمَّانَ
Listen to the student carefully so that they are pronouncing the all the strong joins properly.
Always listen to the student read without spelling first, and then ask the student to spell random words so you are able to assess their progress accurately.

Alif with a small Saad on top ٱ is silent and will be ignored.

EXERCISE 02 & 03   Dual words (Consecutive strong joins)

The student must be confident in reading Shaddah letters when written in dual and plural words: وَكَلَّمَ ٱللَّهُ
Listen to the student carefully so that they are pronouncing all the strong joins properly.
Always listen to the student read without spelling first, and then ask the student to spell random words so you are able to assess their progress accurately.

Alif with a small Saad on top ٱ is silent and will be ignored.

LESSON 18 — SHADDAH

رَبْ + بَ = رَبَّ   قَلْ + لَ = قَلَّ   أَنْ + نَ = أَنَّ

إِنَّ   ثُمَّ   عَمَّ   مَنَّ   مَدَّ   حَجَّ   تَبَّ   ظَنَّ

صَبَّ   مِمَّ   أَيِّ   شَرِّ   صَلِّ   مِتُّ   قَلَّ   رَبَّ

شَقَّا   حُبًّا   دَكًّا   حَقٌّ   غَمٌّ   ضُرٍّ   كُلٌّ   لُدًّا

صَفًّا   غِلٍّ   حِلٌّ   جَمًّا   أُمٌّ   ظِلٍّ   فَجٍّ   عِزًّا

يَمُدُّ   جَنَّةٍ   كَرَّةٌ   أُمَّةٍ   يَفِرُّ   يَحُضُّ

جِثِيًّا   فَرِيًّا   هَيِّنْ   بُكِيًّا   سُجَّدًا   خَرُّوا

هَمَّتْ   تَبَّتْ   حُقَّتْ   مُتُّمْ   خَفَّتْ   تَخَلَّتْ

تَقَبَّلْ   كَذَّبَتْ   زُوِّجَتْ   عُطِّلَتْ   أُقِّتَتْ   أُجِّلَتْ

    Completed on   /   /

- ▸ Read the words that include a Shaddah letter without any hesitation. E.g. Rab-ba رَبّ, Qal-la قَلّ, An-na أَنّ.

- ▸ Spell the words which include a Shaddah letter. E.g.

Step 1	Ra-Ba Fat-hah = Rab	رَبْ
Step 2	Ba-Fat-hah = Ba	بَ
Step 3	Read the entire word, Rab-ba	رَبَّ

- ▸ Shaddah is actually two letters in one.
- ▸ Any time you see a Shaddah (ّ) you make a strong join.

- ◉ I can read and spell the words that include a Shaddah fluently.
- ◉ I can read each line fluently (without hesitation or pausing).
- ◉ I can implement all the lessons learnt previously into this exercise.

EXERCISE 01 — DOUBLE SHADDAH WORDS

يُكَذِّبُ	صَبِيًّا	بَغِيًّا	جِبِلًّا	نُقَدِّسُ	تُحَدِّثُ
مُتَّقِينَ	مُصَلِّينَ	ٱلْأَوَّلِينَ	وَٱلنَّاسِ	وَدَّعَكَ	بِأَنَّهُمْ

يُبَيِّنُ	يَخْتَصُّ	أَنَاسِيَّ	مُصَدِّقًا	نُيَسِّرُ	يُبَدِّلُ
مُنْفَكِّينَ	إِنْسِيًّا	فِيهِنَّ	مَقْضِيًّا	مَرْضِيًّا	شَرْقِيًّا

يَتَوَفَّهُنَّ	ذُرِّيَّتَهُ	وَٱلرُّمَّانَ	وَٱلنَّبِيِّينَ	أُمِّيُّونَ	
بِٱلسَّيِّئَةِ	لَيُبَطِّئَنَّ	وَلَيُمَكِّنَنَّ	فَلَنَقُصَّنَّ	فَلَنُنَبِّئَنَّ	

يَشَّقَّقُ	فَلْيُغَيِّرُنَّ	لَأَتَّخِذَنَّ	لِلسَّيَّارَةِ	وَلَا ٱلسَّيِّئَةُ
وَلَيَمَسَّنَّكُمْ	وَٱلصِّدِّيقِينَ	ٱلرَّبَّانِيُّونَ	لَأُمَنِّيَنَّهُمْ	يَضَّرَّعُونَ

STEP BY STEP

→ Read and spell the words that include **two Shaddah** letters fluently.

Step		
Step 1	Ta Dhammah = Tu	تُ
Step 2	Ha-Daal Fat-hah = Had	حَدَّ
Step 3	Join the two letters = Tu-Had	تُحَدَّ
Step 4	Daal Kasrah = De	دِ
Step 5	Join all previous = Tu-Had-De	تُحَدِّ
Step 6	Tha Dhammah = Thu	ثُ
Step 7	Read the entire word = Tu-Had-De-Thu	تُحَدِّثُ

QUICK TIPS

Imagine the Shaddah letter is sticky, so whatever you join onto it sticks to it.

Note: The Hamzah will be written in the middle of Laam and Alif لَا تَيْنَهُمْ *, you will stretch the Hamzah because of the Alif.*

The small floating Ya (Madd Kasrah) is sometimes written on the Ya وَٱلنَّبِيِّنَ *this indicates that the Ya with a Kasrah before it will be stretched.*

CHECKLIST

- ✓ I can read and spell the words that have two Shaddah's fluently
- ✓ I can read each line fluently (without hesitation or pausing).
- ✓ I can implement all the lessons learnt previously into this exercise.

Comments

EXERCISE 02 — DUAL WORDS

فَمَنْ ٱللَّهُ	أَضَلَّ ٱللَّهُ	فَضَّلَ ٱللَّهُ	وَكَلَّمَ ٱللَّهُ	إِلَّا ٱلظَّنَّ
وَلِيَ ٱللَّهُ	إِلَّا ٱلْحَقَّ	مَدَّ ٱلظِّلَّ	كُلَّ مُمَزَّقٍ	أَحَلَّ ٱللَّهُ
وَلِيُّكُمُ ٱللَّهُ	عَلَّمَكُمُ ٱللَّهُ	وَٱتَّبَعَ مِلَّةَ	كُلَّمَا رُدُّوا	
وَيُحِقُّ ٱلْحَقَّ	لَعَلَّهُمْ يَتَّقُونَ	ذُرِّيَّةً طَيِّبَةً	فَبَرَّأَهُ ٱللَّهُ	
وَإِنَّا لَنَظُنُّكَ	حُيِّيتُمْ بِتَحِيَّةٍ	ثُمَّ صَوَّرْنَٰكُمْ	وَأَشَدَّ قُوَّةً	
وَأُمُّهُۥ صِدِّيقَةٌ	إِنَّ ٱلْعِزَّةَ لِلَّهِ	مُحِلِّي ٱلصَّيْدِ	ثُمَّ لَآتِيَنَّهُم	
يَتَوَلَّى ٱلصَّٰلِحِينَ	أَكَّٰلُونَ لِلسُّحْتِ	ٱلْأَنفُسُ ٱلشُّحَّ	يَقُصُّ ٱلْحَقَّ	
وَقَدَّرَ فِي ٱلسَّرْدِ	فَإِنَّهَا مُحَرَّمَةٌ	هُوَ عَلَىَّ هَيِّنٌ	سُنَّتَ ٱلْأَوَّلِينَ	

STEP BY STEP

- ▶ Read the dual and plural words that include a Shaddah in each word.
- ▶ Spell the dual and plural words that include a Shaddah in each word.

Step 1	Alif-Laam Kasrah = Il	إِلَّا
Step 2	Laam-Dhaa Fat-hah = Ladh	لَّا ٱلظَّ
Step 3	Join the two letters = Il-Ladh	إِلَّا ٱلظَّ
Step 4	Dhaa-Noon Fat-hah = Dhan	ظَّنَ
Step 5	Join all previous = Il-Ladh-Dhan	إِلَّا ٱلظَّنَ
Step 6	Noon Fat-hah = Na	نَّ
Step 7	Join all previous = Il-Ladh-Dhan-Na	إِلَّا ٱلظَّنَّ

QUICK TIPS

- ◆ Two words with two sticky letters.
- ◆ Before reading it, point out the Shaddahs, so when you read it you can apply the Shaddahs at the right place.

CHECKLIST

- ✓ I can read and spell the dual words that have Shaddah fluently.
- ✓ I can read each line fluently (without hesitation or pausing).
- ✓ I can implement all the lessons learnt previously into this exercise.

EXERCISE 03 — DUAL WORDS — س س

إِنَّ ٱلَّذِينَ	فَٱلصَّٰلِحَٰتُ	مِنَ ٱلطَّيِّبَٰتِ	إِلَّا ٱلَّذِينَ	
إِنَّ ٱلسَّاعَةَ	فَلَهُنَّ ٱلثُّمُنُ	رَبُّ ٱلشِّعْرَىٰ	فَلَمَّا تَغَشَّىٰهَا	
فَلِأُمِّهِ ٱلثُّلُثُ	وَيُوَلُّونَ ٱلدُّبُرَ	وَقَرَّبْنَٰهُ نَجِيًّا	بِٱلَّيْلِ وَٱلنَّهَارِ	
ٱلنُّبُوَّةَ	ذُرِّيَّتِهِمَا	عَلَّمَكُمُ ٱلسِّحْرَ	وَإِذَا مَسَّهُ ٱلشَّرُّ	وَسَخَّرَ ٱلشَّمْسَ

ٱلطَّيِّبَٰتُ لِلطَّيِّبِينَ	يُقَلِّبُ كَفَّيْهِ	فَٱتَّخِذُوهُ عَدُوًّا
يُنسِيَنَّكَ ٱلشَّيْطَٰنُ	لَا تُكَلَّفُ إِلَّا نَفْسَكَ	إِذْ يُغَشِّيكُمُ ٱلنُّعَاسَ
يَتَّبِعُونَ ٱلشَّهَوَٰتِ	لَا تَتَّبِعُمُ ٱلشَّيْطَٰنَ	وَمَا عَلَّمْنَٰهُ ٱلشِّعْرَ
أَوْ لَتَعُودُنَّ فِي مِلَّتِنَا	وَٱلسَّارِقُ وَٱلسَّارِقَةُ	وَيُحِبُّهُمْ وَيُحِبُّونَهُ

STEP BY STEP

↠ Read and spell the dual and plural words that include Shaddah letters in them fluently.

Step		
Step 1	Alif-Laam Kasrah = Il	إِلّ
Step 2	Laam-Laam Fat-hah = Lal	لَّ آلّ
Step 3	Join the two letters = Il-Lal	إِلَّ آلّ
Step 4	La Fat-hah = La	لَ
Step 5	Join all previous = Il-Lal-La	إِلَّ آلَّ
Step 6	Thaal Ya Kasrah = Thee	ذِي
Step 7	Join all previous = Il-Lal-La-Thee	إِلَّ آلَّذِي
Step 8	Noon Fat-hah = Na	نَ
Step 9	Read the entire word = Il-Lal-La-Thee-Na	إِلَّ آلَّذِينَ

QUICK TIPS

↠ **Do not stretch** Fat-hah, Kasrah and Dhammah letters.
Split the long words into smaller chunks, practice them and then read them together.

CHECKLIST

- I can **read and spell** the dual and plural words that have Shaddah in them fluently.
- I can read each line fluently (without hesitation or pausing).
- I can implement all the lessons learnt previously into this exercise.

The Prophet ﷺ said:

"The best amongst you is he who learns the Qur'aan and teaches it to others."

(Muslim)

OVERVIEW

LESSON 19 > SILENT LETTERS IN WORDS

If a letter appears in a word without a Harakah, it will not be pronounced or even spelt. These are called **'Silent Letters'** which are generally **'Alif', 'Waw' and 'Ya'**.
They have been highlighted in red on the first two lines.
- Silent Alif is normally written between two words.
- Silent Waw is normally written in the middle of the word.
- Silent Ya is normally written at the end of the word.

LESSON 20 > SILENT ALIF

Whenever an Alif comes with a **small circle above it,** it will be ignored. There are some words in the Qur'aan that include this silent Alif and have been mentioned in this lesson.

LESSON 21 > SPECIAL WORDS

There are only 3 words in the Qur'aan that have both the **'Seen'** and **'Saad'** together.
Whenever the letter Ta comes after the Seen or Saad, then Seen will be read.
- The letters that are to be read are in green and the ones that are not supposed to be read are in red.
- There is one word in the Qur'aan that has a dot beneath the Ra, this indicates a Madd kasrah but is pronounced in a **different manner**.

LESSON 22 > WORDS WITH A JERKING SOUND

If a Hamzah with a Sukoon appears on an **Alif, Waw or Ya,** the letters Alif, Waw and Ya, **will be ignored** and the Hamzah will be read with a slight jerking sound.
The student should always read each line without hesitation or pausing to help build consistency and speed.

LESSON 19: SILENT LETTERS IN WORDS

أُوىٰ

كَفَىٰ	أَبَىٰ	أَتَىٰ	إِلَىٰ	عَلَىٰ
ضُحًّى	أَبْقَىٰ	ءَاوَىٰ	سُدًى	هَوَىٰ
أَخْفَىٰ	يَحْيَىٰ	طَغَىٰ	سُوَّىٰ	هَدَىٰ
تَنْسَىٰ	فَأَوْحَىٰ	صَلَوٰةً	أُخْرَىٰ	تَرْقَىٰ
لِتَشْقَىٰ	فَتُلْقَىٰ	كُسَالَىٰ	تَرْضَىٰ	زَكَوٰةً

يَشْوِى ٱلْوُجُوهَ	عَلَى ٱلْإِنْسَٰنِ	زَهَقَ ٱلْبَاطِلُ	قُرْءَانَ ٱلْفَجْرِ
ذِى ٱلْقَرْنَيْنِ	هُنَالِكَ ٱلْوَلَايَةُ	وَزِدْنَٰهُمْ هُدًى	يَٰمُوسَىٰ مَسْحُورًا
عَلَى ٱلْعَرْشِ ٱسْتَوَىٰ	مَا ٱسْتَطَٰعُوا۟ لَهُۥ	يَوْمَ ٱلْقِيَٰمَةِ أَعْمَىٰ	فَتَرَى ٱلْمُجْرِمِينَ

STEP BY STEP

•▶ Read the words that include a silent letter.
E.g. 'Alaa عَلَا, Elaa إِلَا, Ataa أَتَا.

•▶ Spell the words which include a **silent letter**. E.g.

Step 1	'Ayn, Fat-hah = 'A	عَ
Step 2	Laam, Madd Fat-hah = Laa	لَا
Step 3	Read the the entire word = 'A-laa	عَلَا

QUICK TIPS

When you see an Alif ا, Waw و or Ya ي without any harakah on them they will be ignored. When the letter after these 3 letters has a Sukoon or Shaddah then letter before will join straight on to the Sukoon or Shaddah letter.

CHECKLIST

☉ I can **read and spell** the **single and double words** that include silent letters.

☉ I can read each line **fluently in one breath** (without hesitation or pausing).

☉ I can implement all the lessons learnt previously into this exercise.

LESSON 20 — SILENT ALIF

أَنَا

نَدْعُوا۟	أَنَا۠ أَخُوكَ	أَنَا۠ عَابِدٌ	أَنَا۠ نَذِيرٌ
لِتَتْلُوا۟	لَٰكِنَّا۠ هُوَ	لِيَرْبُوا۟	ثَمُودَا۠

سَلَٰسِلَا۠	أَفَإِنْ	وَمَلَإِي۠هِۦ	لِيَبْلُوا۟
وَنَبْلُوَا۟ أَخْبَارَكُمْ	لَا۠ إِلَى ٱلْجَحِيمِ	وَلَا۠ أَوْضَعُوا۟	قَوَارِيرَا۠

STEP BY STEP

• ▶ Read the words that include a silent Alif.
E.g. Ana أَنَا۠ , Ana-natheeroon أَنَا۠ نَذِيرٌ ,
Ana-'Aabi-doon أَنَا۠ عَابِدٌ .

• ▶ Spell the words which include a **silent Alif** fluently. E.g.

Step 1	Alif Fat-hah = A	أَ
Step 2	Noon Fat-hah = Na	نَا۠
Step 3	Read the entire word, A-na	أَنَا۠

When a small circle comes on an Alif أَنَا۠ it cancels it.

QUICK TIPS

CHECKLIST

◉ I can **read and spell** the words that include the silent Alif.

◉ I can read each line fluently in one breath (without hesitation or pausing).

◉ I can implement all the lessons learnt previously into this exercise.

LESSON 21: SPECIAL WORDS

Surah Al Baqarah.

Surah Al A'raaf.

Surah At Toor.

Identify which letters to read in these **three** words that include "Seen" and "Saad".

Pronounce the sound of the letter Ra "Maj-ray-haa". The letter "Ra" will be pronounced like the word "Rare" in English.

Completed on   /   /

STEP BY STEP

• ▶ Read the words that include a Seen and Saad.
E.g. Wa-yab-sutu وَيَبْصُطُ , Basta-tan بَصْطَةً ,
Humul-musaytiroona هُمُ ٱلْمُصَيْطِرُونَ .

• ▶ Spell the words that include a Seen and Saad. E.g.

Step 1	Waw, Fat-hah = Wa	وَ
Step 2	Ya, Ba, Fat-hah = Yab	يَبْ
Step 3	Join the two words, Wa-Yab	وَيَبْ
Step 4	Seen, Dhammah = Su	صُ
Step 5	Join all previous, Wa-Yab-Su	وَيَبْصُ
Step 6	Ta, Dhammah = Tu	طُ
Step 7	Read the entire word, Wa-Yab-Su-Tu	وَيَبْصُطُ

If after the letters Seen & Saad the letter Ta ط comes, the letter Seen س will be read not Saad. E.g. وَيَبْصُطُ

QUICK TIPS

CHECKLIST

◉ I can **read and spell** the words which have the letters **Seen and Saad**.

◉ I can read each line **fluently in one breath** (without hesitation or pausing).

◉ I can implement all the lessons learnt previously into this exercise.

Comments

LESSON 22 — WORDS WITH A JERKING SOUND

يَأْبَ بَأْسٍ نَأْتِ كَأْسًا شَأْنٌ

وَأْمُرْ وَرِئْيًا وَلُؤْلُؤًا يُؤْمِنُ قَرَأْتَ

يُؤْتِيَنِ أَخْطَأْتُمْ جِئْتُكُمْ يُؤْفَكُ يُؤْذَنُ

مَأْوَاهُمْ تُؤْثِرُونَ مُؤْصَدَةٌ فَيُؤْخَذُ أَيَأْمُرُكُمْ

وَهُوَ مُؤْمِنٌ بَلْ تُؤْثِرُونَ مَا يُؤْمَرُونَ لَا يَسْتَأْخِرُونَ

يَأْكُلْ مِنْهَا أَبْلِغْهُ مَأْمَنَهُ وَكَأْسًا دِهَاقًا تَأْكُلُوا جَمِيعًا

فَأْتِيَا فِرْعَوْنَ وَلِلْأَرْضِ ائْتِيَا يَأْتِينِي بِعَرْشِهَا لَقَدْ جِئْتِ شَيْئًا

يُؤْتِيهِمْ أُجُورَهُمْ يَأْجُوجَ وَمَأْجُوجَ وَأْتُونِي مُسْلِمِينَ يَأْلَمُونَ كَمَا تَأْلَمُونَ

- ▶ Read the words that have Hamzah with a Sukoon above them fluently.
  E.g. Ya'ba يَأْبَ , Ba'sin بَأْسٍ , Na'te نَأْتِ .

- ▶ Spell the words that include a Hamzah with a Sukoon E.g.

Step 1	Ya, Hamzah, Fat-hah = Ya'	يَأْ
Step 2	Ba, Fat-hah = Ba	بَ
Step 3	Read the entire word, Ya'-ba	يَأْبَ

QUICK TIPS

If Hamzah comes with a Sukoon on an Alif, Waw or Ya. The Alif, Waw or Ya will become silent and will be read with a slight jerking sound يَأْبَ .

CHECKLIST

- ☑ I can read and spell the words with a jerking sound which have a **Sukoon above a Hamzah** and a **Sukoon above a silent Alif** fluently.

- ☑ I can read each line **fluently in one breath** (without hesitation or pausing).

- ☑ I can implement all the lessons learnt previously into this exercise.

GRADE 11

The Prophet ﷺ said:
"The one who was devoted to the Qur'aan will be told on the Day of Resurrection: "Recite and ascend (in ranks) as you used to recite when you were in the world. Your rank will be at the last Ayah you recite."
(Abu Dawud and Tirmidhi)

OVERVIEW

Small Madd is to stretch for 2 seconds

- ❯ The small Madd indicates that the letter will be stretched for around two seconds.
- ❯ A small Madd is always in need of a Harakah before it. It can never come by itself rather it stretches the sound of the Harakah before it.
- ❯ E.g. If a Fat-hah comes before a small madd, the sound of the Fat-hah will be stretched.
- ❯ Ensure the student is confident in spelling this lesson.

Big Madd is to stretch for 4 seconds

- ❯ The Big Madd indicates the letter will be stretched for around 3 to 4 seconds.
- ❯ A Big Madd is always in need of a Harakah before it. It can never come by itself rather it stretches the sound of the Harakah before it.
- ❯ E.g. If a Fat-hah comes before a Big madd, the sound of the Fat-hah will be stretched.
- ❯ Ensure the student is confident in spelling this lesson.

Stretch followed by a strong join

- ❯ If after a Big Madd a Shaddah appears , then you must stretch and do a strong join for around 3 to 4 seconds: جَآنّ
- ❯ Ensure the student is confident in spelling this lesson.

LESSON 23 — SMALL MADD

إِلَّا إِذَا	حَتَّىٰ إِذَا	إِنَّمَا أَنَا۠	إِلَىٰ أُمِّهِۦ
وَلَا أَقُولُ	بِمَا أَنزَلَ	أَبًا أَحَدٍ	إِنَّا ءَامَنَّا
فَلَهُۥ أَسْلِمُوا	لَمَّا ءَاتَيْتُكُم	إِلَىٰ أَنفُسِهِمْ	لَهُۥ أَصْحَبُ
يَٰٓإِبْرَٰهِيمُ	لَهُۥ أَهْلَهُۥ	فَإِذَآ أُوذِىَ	إِنِّى أَحْبَبْتُ

فَلَآ أُقْسِمُ بِٱلشَّفَقِ — إِنَّ إِلَيْنَآ إِيَابَهُمْ

فَيَقُولُ رَبِّىٓ أَكْرَمَنِ — لَا يَصْلَىٰهَآ إِلَّا ٱلْأَشْقَى

لَآ أَعْبُدُ مَا تَعْبُدُونَ — ٱلَّذِىٓ أَنقَضَ ظَهْرَكَ

وَمَآ أَدْرَىٰكَ مَا سِجِّينٌ — وَٱلَّذِىٓ أَخْرَجَ ٱلْمَرْعَىٰ

STEP BY STEP

• Read the words that include a small Madd fluently. E.g. Il-laaa-Ithaa إِلَإِذَا , Hat-Taaa-Ithaa أَئِنَّا أَنَّا , In-namaaa-ana حَتَّى إِذَا .

• Spell the words which include a small Madd E.g.

Step 1	Alif, Laam Kasrah = Il	إِلْ
Step 2	Laam, Alif Fat-hah, Madd = Laaa	لَا
Step 3	Join the two, Il-Laaa	إِلَا
Step 4	Alif, Kasrah = E	إِ
Step 5	Join all previous, Il-Laaa-E	إِلَإِ
Step 6	Thaal, Alif, Fat-hah = Thaa	ذَا
Step 7	Read the entire word, Il-Laaa-E-Thaa	إِلَإِذَا

QUICK TIPS

• Stretch the small Madd for 2 seconds.

• Madd normally comes on a letter that is already stretched. The letter with a Madd on it will be stretched for 2 seconds or so in total.

CHECKLIST

✓ I can **read and spell** the words that include a **small Madd** fluently.

✓ I can read **each line fluently** (without hesitation or pausing).

✓ I can implement all the lessons learnt previously into this exercise.

Comments

LESSON 24: BIG MADD

بِلِقَآءِ	يَشَآءُ	دُعَآءِ	ءَابَآءِ
وَضِيَآءً	إِيتَآءِ	تَبُوَّأَ	يُضِيٓءُ
شُهَدَآءَ	هَنِيٓئًا	شَعَآئِرَ	سَيْنَآءَ
لِلطَّآئِفِينَ	أَدْعِيَآئِهِمْ	وَأَحِبَّآؤُهُ	قَآئِلُهَا

أَسَآءُوا السُّوٓءَىٰ	لَآ أَتَّبِعُ أَهْوَآءَكُمْ
أَلَا سَآءَ مَايَحْكُمُونَ	يَوْمَ نَطْوِى السَّمَآءَ
أَلَآ إِنَّ أَوْلِيَآءَ اللَّهِ	يَوْمَ تُبْلَى السَّرَآئِرُ
ءَابَآءَنَا الضَّرَّآءُ وَالسَّرَّآءُ	بَوَّأْنَا بَنِىٓ إِسْرَآئِيلَ

- Read the words that include a **big Madd** fluently. E.g. Aa-baaa-e عَابَآءِ , Du-'Aaaa-e دُعَآءَ , Ya-shaaa-o يَشَآءُ .

- Spell the words which include a **big Madd** E.g.

Step 1	Hamzah, Alif, Fat-hah = Aa	ءَا
Step 2	Ba, Alif, Fat-hah, Madd = Baaa	بَآ
Step 3	Join the two, Aa-Baaa	عَابَآ
Step 4	Hamzah, Kasrah = E	ءِ
Step 5	Read the entire word, Aa-Baaa-E	عَابَآءِ

- Stretch the big Madd for 3 to 4 seconds. (Same as small Madd but longer stretch).

Note: Small Madd and big Madd look the same, the stretch is different.

- I can **read and spell** the dual words that have a **small** and **big** Madd fluently.
- I can read **each line fluently** (without hesitation or pausing).
- I can implement all the lessons learnt previously into this exercise.

LESSON 25: BIG MADD FOLLOWED BY A SHADDAH

كَافَّةً	ءَآللَّهُ	ضَآلًّا	جَآنٌّ
شَآقُّوا	خَآصَّةً	ءَآمِّينَ	دَآبَّةٍ
ظَآنِّينَ	تَتَّبِعَنِّ	حَآجَّكَ	بِرَآدِّى
أَتُحَآجُّونِّى	ءَآلذَّكَرَيْنِ	تَحَٰضُّونَ	ضَآلِّينَ

لَرَآدُّكَ إِلَىٰ مَعَادٍ	إِنَّا رَآدُّوهُ إِلَيْكِ
فَإِذَا جَآءَتِ ٱلصَّآخَّةُ	إِنَّ هَٰٓؤُلَآءِ لَضَآلُّونَ
يُوَآدُّونَ مَنْ حَآدَّ ٱللَّهَ	أَلْحَآقَّةُ مَا ٱلْحَآقَّةُ
إِنَّ ٱلَّذِينَ يُحَآدُّونَ ٱللَّهَ	إِنْسٌ قَبْلَهُمْ وَلَا جَآنٌّ

   Completed on / /

STEP BY STEP

- ▸ Read the words that include a big Madd followed by a Shaddah letter fluently. E.g. Jaaan-nun جَآنّ , Dhaaal-lan ضَآلّ , Aaaal-laahu ءَآللَّهُ .

- ▸ Spell the words which include a big Madd followed by a Shaddah letter E.g.

Step 1	Jeem, Noon, Fat-hah, Madd = Jaaann	جَآنّ
Step 2	Noon, Dhamma-tayn = Nun	نٌ
Step 3	Read the entire word, Jaaann-Nun	جَآنّ

- ▸ Stretch the sound for around 3 to 4 seconds and join straight onto the Shaddah letter.

- ▸ Ensure a strong join is done instantly after a long stretch.

QUICK TIPS

CHECKLIST

- ✓ I can **read and spell** the words that include a big **Madd followed by a Shaddah** letter fluently.

- ✓ I can read **each line fluently** (without any hesitation or pausing).

- ✓ I can implement all the lessons learnt previously into this exercise.

GRADE 12

The Prophet ﷺ said:

"Whoever recites a letter from the Book of Allaah, he will be credited with a good deed, and a good deed gets a ten-fold reward. I do not say that Alif-Laam-Meem is one letter, but Alif is a letter, Laam is a letter and Meem is a letter."

(Muslim)

OVERVIEW

LESSON 26 > QALQALAH

Qalqalah is to pronounce a letter with an echo sound

- When any of the letters of Qalqalah ق ط ب ج د appear with a Sukoon, the letter will be read with a slight echo.
- The same rule will apply if any of these letters come at the end of a word.

LESSON 27 > GHUNNAH

Ghunnah means to stretch with a deep nasal sound

- When a **Noon** نّ or **Meem** مّ appears with a **Shaddah**, the sound will be stretched in the nose for 1-2 seconds.

LESSON 28 > IZHAAR

Izhaar is to read the Noon saakin or Tanween clearly without any nasal stretching sound

- To read the sound of the **Noon saakin or Tanween** clearly (without Ghunnah).
- If after a **Noon Saakin** or **Tanween** any of these 6 throat letters appear ع ح خ ه غ there will be Izhaar, i.e. No Ghunnah.

Note: Tanween = Fat-ha-tayn, Kasra-tayn and Dhamma-tayn ًـ ٍـ ٌـ .

LESSON 26: QALQALAH

وَعَدْلًا	أَقْلَامٌ	أَطْهَرُ	عِجْلًا	عَبْدًا
أَعْتَدْنَا	بِقِطْعٍ	يَطْبَعُ	نَجْعَل	إِذْهَب
فَاْخْرُجْ	أُقْسِمُ	فَاهْبِطْ	تَجْهَرُ	أَبْصَرَ
صَدْرِي	أَقْلِعِي	بِعِجْلٍ	خَطْبُكَ	يَبْسُطْ
مَقْطُوعٌ	تَجْعَلُ	صَدْرُكَ	يَبْنُؤُمَّ	تُسْقِطْ
تَبْتَئِسْ	يَلْتَقِطْهُ	تَدْمِيرًا	لِتُبْدِى	فَاجْتَبَهُ
تُعَذِّبْهُم	وَاجْتَبَيْنَا	تَبْسُطْهَا	أَوِ اطْرَحُوهُ	أَحْرَقْتَهَا
تُطْعِمُونَ	رَزَقْنَاكُمْ	حَسِبْتُمْ	مُجْرِمُونَ	خَلَقْنَاكُمْ

STEP BY STEP

•▶ Read the words which include a Qalqalah fluently

•▶ Spell the words which include a Qalqalah (refer to Lesson 06: Sukoon).

•▶ Identify the Qalqalah letters confidently

Qalqalah is to read a letter with a slight bounce

QUICK TIPS

•▶ Make sure the bounce of the Qalqalah is only a third of a Fat-hah sound.

•▶ Remember this one word *Qutubujad*, it has all the letters of Qalqalah ق ط ب ج د , which should help you remember them.
Qu-tu-bu-jad = قُطْبُجَدُ

CHECKLIST

- ☑ I can **read and spell** the words that include a **Qalqalah** properly.
- ☑ I can read **each line fluently** (without hesitation or pausing).
- ☑ I can implement all the lessons learnt previously into this exercise.

LESSON 27 — GHUNNAH

كُنَّا	تَمَّتْ	عَنَّا	مِمَّا	جَنَّ
صُمٌّ	وَجَنَّتٍ	وَلَمَّا	ءَامَنَّا	هَلُمَّ
لَتَعُودُنَّ	أُمَّةٌ	جَهَنَّمَ	عَمَّا	فِيهِنَّ
أَئِمَّةً	فَلَنَسْئَلَنَّ	وَأُمِّي	لَيَمَسَّنَّ	غُمَّةً
لَنَكُونَنَّ	وَهَمُّوا	وَالنَّبِيِّـۧنَ	ذِمَّةً	لَنَظُنُّكَ
لَأَمْلَأَنَّ	ٱلْأُمِّيِّـۧنَ	لَآتِيَنَّهُمْ	أَهَمَّتْهُمْ	مَكَّنَّـٰكُمْ
لَيُؤْمِنَنَّ	فَعُمِّيَتْ	لَيَزِيدَنَّ	فَأَتِمُّوا	فَلَنَقُصَّنَّ
يُنْسِيَنَّكَ	سَمَّعُونَ	فَتَيَمَّمُوا	مُتَعَمِّدًا	لَايَفْتِنَنَّكُمْ

• Read the words that include a Ghunnah

• Spell the words which include a Ghunnah (refer to Lesson 10: Shaddah).

• Identify the Ghunnah letters confidently.

Ghunnah is to stretch with a strong nasal sound

Do a Ghunnah (strong nasal sound) when you see the letters مّ **and** نّ .

Note: The Hamzah will be written in the middle of Laam and Alif اَلَّا تَيْنَهُمْ , *this will mean you will **stretch the Hamzah** because of the Alif.*
The small floating Ya (Madd Kasrah) is written on the Ya وَٱلنَّبِيِّـۧنَ *and means that the Kasrah before it will be stretched.*

- I can **read and spell** the words that **include a Ghunnah** properly.
- I can read **each line fluently** (without hesitation or pausing).
- I can implement all the lessons learnt previously into this exercise.

LESSON 28 — IZHAAR

| مِنْ هَادٍ | مَنْ عَمِلَ | مِنْ حَرَجٍ | مِنْ خَوْفٍ |

| مَنْ أَعْطَى | وَمِنْ خِزْيِ | يَوْمٌ عَسِرٌ | عَذَابًا أَلِيمًا |

| مَثَلًا عَبْدًا | لِيَوْمٍ عَظِيمٍ | حُورٌ عِينٌ | حَكِيمٍ خَبِيرٍ |

| لَا خَوْفٌ عَلَيْهِمْ | وَإِنْ عَاقَبْتُمْ | نَارٌ حَامِيَةٌ | وَلِمَنْ خَافَ |

| كَلِمَةٍ خَبِيثَةٍ | أُمَّةٍ أَجَلٌ | شَفَاعَةً حَسَنَةً | قُرْءَانًا أَعْجَمِيًّا |

| كَذَّابٌ أَشِرٌ | مِنْ أَقْطَارِهَا | بَيَاتًا أَوْ نَهَارًا | طَيْرًا أَبَابِيلَ |

| مِنْ عَيْنٍ ءَانِيَةٍ | أَشِحَّةً عَلَيْكُمْ | فِي يَوْمٍ عَاصِفٍ | وَلَا تَحْزَنْ عَلَيْهِمْ |

| خَيْرَاتٌ حِسَانٌ | وَعَبْقَرِيٍّ حِسَانٍ | بِسَلَامٍ ءَامِنِينَ | مُخْتَلِفًا أَلْوَانُهُ |

- Read the words that include a Izhaar

- Spell the words that include a Izhaar (refer to Lesson 06: Sukoon)

- Identify the **Throat letters** confidently

Izhaar is to read the Noon Saakin or Tanween clearly without any nasal stretching sound

Izhaar is to read the Noon Saakin نْ and Tanween ـٌ ـٍ ـً clearly, i.e. without Ghunnah.

- I can **read and spell** the words that **include Izhaar** properly.
- I can read each line **fluently in one breath** (without hesitation or pausing).
- I can implement all the lessons learnt previously into this exercise.

GRADE 13

The Prophet ﷺ said:

"Any group of people that assemble in one of the Houses of Allaah to recite the Book of Allaah, learning and teaching it, tranquility will descend upon them, mercy will engulf them, angels will surround them and Allaah will make mention of them to those (the angels) in His proximity."

(Muslim)

OVERVIEW

LESSON 29 — RULE OF THE LETTER RA

Full mouth with ◌َ and ◌ُ

- Ra with a Fat-hah رَ or Dhammah رُ will be read with a full mouth sound (the same rule applies if the Ra has a Shaddah on it).
- Ra with a Kasrah رِ will be read with an empty mouth sound.
- If Ra has a Sukoon on it and a Fat-hah تَرْ or Dhammah يُرْ is joining onto it, then the letter Ra will be read with a full mouth sound.
- However, if a Kasrah is joining onto it شِرْ , then the letter Ra will be read with an empty mouth.
- The green colour indicates the full mouth Ra and the red colour indicates the empty mouth Ra.

LESSON 30 — RULE OF THE WORD ALLAAH

Full mouth with ◌َ and ◌ُ

- If a Fat-hah or Dhammah is joining onto the word Allaah then the letter Laam in the word Allaah will be pronounced with a full mouth sound: أَمْرُ ٱللَّهِ أَللَّهُ
- If a Kasrah is joining onto the word Allaah, then the letter Laam in the word Allaah will be pronounced with an empty mouth sound: يَرْفَعُ ٱللَّهُ
- The green colour indicates the full mouth Laam and the red colour indicates the empty mouth Laam.

LESSON 29: RULE OF THE LETTER 'RA'

تَرْهَقُهَا قَتَرَةٌ	فَٱلْمُورِيَٰتِ قَدْحًا	فِيهِ ٱلرَّحْمَةُ
مَرْفُوعَةٍ مُطَهَّرَةٍ	يُرْسِلُ ٱلرِّيَٰحَ	لِسَعْيِهَا رَاضِيَةٌ
فَأَكْرَمَهُۥ وَنَعَّمَهُۥ	خَلَقَهُۥ فَقَدَّرَهُۥ	مِنْ ضَرِيعٍ
رُءُوسَكُمْ وَمُقَصِّرِينَ	وَإِلَىٰ رَبِّكَ فَٱرْغَبْ	فِى صُحُفٍ مُكَرَّمَةٍ
فَرَوْحٌ وَّرَيْحَانٌ	عُرُبًا أَتْرَابًا	رِيحًا صَرْصَرًا
فِيهَا سُرُرٌ مَّرْفُوعَةٌ	كُلُّ أَمْرٍ مُسْتَقِرٌّ	فَٱلزَّٰجِرَٰتِ زَجْرًا
كُلُّ شِرْبٍ مُحْتَضَرٌ	إِنَّ مَعَ ٱلْعُسْرِ يُسْرًا	هَٰذَا عَارِضٌ مُمْطِرُنَا
أُولَٰئِكَ هُمْ خَيْرُ ٱلْبَرِيَّةِ	فَقَدَرَ عَلَيْهِ رِزْقَهُۥ	فَشَٰرِبُونَ شُرْبَ ٱلْهِيمِ

- Read the letter **Ra** as a **full mouth letter** when it has a **Fat-hah** or **Dhammah** above it

- Read the letter **Ra** as an **empty mouth letter** when it has a **Kasrah** beneath it

The letter Ra will be read with a full mouth when it comes with a ◌َ or ◌ُ

QUICK TIPS

Fat-hah ◌َ & Dhammah ◌ُ = Full mouth
Kasrah ◌ِ = Empty mouth

CHECKLIST

- I can read the letter **Ra** as a **full mouth letter**.
- I can read **each line fluently** (without hesitation or pausing).
- I can implement all the lessons learnt previously into this exercise.

LESSON 30: RULE OF THE WORD ALLAAH

حُرُمَتِ ٱللَّهِ	كَتَبَ ٱللَّهُ	يَرْفَعِ ٱللَّهُ	حِزْبُ ٱللَّهِ
لِذِكْرِ ٱللَّهِ	أَمْرُ ٱللَّهِ	يُشَآقِّ ٱللَّهَ	وَعَدَ ٱللَّهُ
غَضِبَ ٱللَّهُ	عَفَا ٱللَّهُ	وَجْهَ ٱللَّهِ	هُوَ ٱللَّهُ
يَهْدِى ٱللَّهُ	أَطِيعُوا۟ ٱللَّهَ	فَٱتَّقُوا۟ ٱللَّهَ	فِى سَبِيلِ ٱللَّهِ
يَبْعَثُهُمُ ٱللَّهُ	ٱعْبُدُوا۟ ٱللَّهَ	أَنْ هَدَىٰنَا ٱللَّهُ	فَيَنسَخُ ٱللَّهُ
أَنِ ٱشْكُرْ لِلَّهِ	عَن ذِكْرِ ٱللَّهِ	مِنْ دُونِ ٱللَّهِ	شَعَآئِرَ ٱللَّهِ
أَعْدَآءِ ٱللَّهِ ٱلنَّارُ	ٱتَّقُوا۟ ٱللَّهَ حَقَّ تُقَاتِهِۦ	قُلْ صَدَقَ ٱللَّهُ	
لِمَ تَكْفُرُونَ بِـَٔايَـٰتِ ٱللَّهِ	يَضْرِبُ ٱللَّهُ ٱلْأَمْثَالَ	وَمَا مِنْ إِلَـٰهٍ إِلَّا ٱللَّهُ	

Completed on / /

- ▸ Read the word Allaah with a full mouth when it has a **Fat-hah** or **Dhammah** before it

- ▸ Read the word Allaah with an **empty mouth** when it has a **Kasrah** before it

The word أَللَّٰه will be read with a full mouth when a ´ or ´ is joining onto it.

Fat-hah ´ & Dhammah ´ = Full mouth
Kasrah ´ = Empty mouth

- ☑ I can read the word **Allaah** with a **full mouth**.
- ☑ I can read **each line fluently** (without hesitation or pausing).
- ☑ I can implement all the lessons learnt previously into this exercise.

GRADE 14

The Prophet ﷺ said:

"Read the Qur'aan, for it will come as an intercessor for its reciters on the Day of Resurrection."

(Muslim)

OVERVIEW

LESSON 31 > IDGHAAM AND SILENT LETTERS

To merge two letters together

- Whenever an **empty letter** and **Shaddah letter** 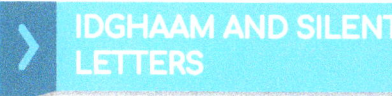 come together, the empty letter will become silent and will not be read or spelt. E.g. The **Kaaf** will join straight onto the **Ta**: كِدتَّ

LESSON 32 > IDGHAAM

Idghaam is to merge two letters together.

- There are 6 letters of Idghaam يرملون
- There are 2 types of Idghaam:
  1. Idghaam without Ghunnah
  2. Idghaam with Ghunnah

Idghaam without Ghunnah

- If after an **empty Noon** or **Tanween** any of these **2 letters** ل & ر appear out of the 6, there will be **Idghaam without Ghunnah**.
- **Idghaam without Ghunnah** means to join directly without any sound in the nose. E.g. The **Fa** joins onto the **Laam** without any sound coming from the nose: أُفِّ لَكُمْ

  Note: Tanween will look slightly different when Idghaam happens.
  Regular Tanween
  Tanween after rules (except Izhaar)

Idghaam with Ghunnah

- If after an **empty Noon** or **Tanween** any of these **4 letters** و م ن ي appear out of the 6, there will be **Idghaam with Ghunnah**.
- **Idghaam with Ghunnah** means to stretch the sound of these letters in the nose when joining. E.g. The **Laam** joins onto the **Ya** but with the sound coming from the nose: رَجُلٌ يُرِيدُ

  Note: Tanween will look slightly different when Idghaam happens.
  Regular Tanween
  Tanween after rules (except Izhaar)

LESSON 31: IDGHAAM AND SILENT LETTERS

بَل رَّفَعَ	عَبَدتُّم	قُل لَّوْ	أَحَطتُ	كِدتَّ	

أَن عَبَدتَّ	أَن رَّبَطنَا	قَد دَّخَلُواْ	بَسَطتَ	أَقُل لَّكَ	

وَعَد تَّهُمْ	وَجَدتُّمْ	لَأَرَدتُّ	قُل رَّبِّ	وُلِدتُّ

وَاذْكُر رَّبَّكَ	فَرَّطتُم	حَصَدتُّمْ	قَد تَّبَيَّنَ	يُدْرِككُّم

إِضْرِب بِّعَصَاكَ	بَل لَّا تُكْرِمُونَ	وَإِن أَرَدتُّمْ	أَلَمْ نَخْلُقكُّم	

وَارْكَب مَّعَنَا	وَقَالَت طَّآئِفَةٌ	رَّبِحَت تِّجَارَتُهُمْ	ءَاوَواْ وَّنَصَرُواْ

STEP BY STEP

→ Read the words which include an **empty** letter and **Shaddah** letter without spelling. E.g.

→ Spell the words which include an **empty letter** and **Shaddah** letter. E.g.

Step 1	Kaaf, Ta, Kasrah = Kit	كِدتْ
Step 2	Ta, Fat-hah = Ta	تَّ
Step 3	Read the entire word, Kit-Ta	كِدتَّ

To merge two letters together by cancelling the letter before the Shaddah letter.

Remember if an empty letter comes before a letter with a Shaddah, it will be cancelled.

QUICK TIPS

CHECKLIST

✓ I can **read and spell** the words that include a **silent letter**.

✓ I can read **each line fluently** (without hesitation or pausing).

✓ I can implement all the lessons learnt previously into this exercise.

LESSON 32 — IDGHAAM WITHOUT GHUNNAH

زَبَدًا رَّابِيًا	جَنَّتٍ لَّهُمْ	نُوحٌ رَّبِّ	أُفٍّ لَّكُمْ
مِن رَّبِّكَ	لَئِن لَّمْ	مَن رَّحِمَ	مِن لَّدُنْهُ
أَخْذَةً رَّابِيَةً	جَمِيعٌ لَّدَيْنَا	عِيدًا لِّأَوَّلِنَا	أَن رَّءَاهُ
عِيشَةٍ رَّاضِيَةٍ	أَن لَّمْ يَرَهُ	مِن رُّسُلِهِ	أَشْتَاتًا لِّيُرَوْا
بَقَرَةٌ لَّا فَارِضٌ	مِن رَّأْسِهِ	مَتَاعًا لَّكُمْ	ثَمَرَةٍ رِّزْقًا
حَقٌّ لِّلسَّائِلِ	لَمْ يَكُن لَّهُ	غَفُورٌ رَّحِيمٌ	تَوَّابٌ رَّحِيمٌ
شِهَابًا رَّصَدًا	خَيْرٌ لِّأَنْفُسِهِمْ	هُدًى لِّلْمُتَّقِينَ	رَءُوفٌ رَّحِيمٌ
مِن رِّزْقِ ٱللَّهِ	كَأَن لَّمْ يَغْنَوْا	خَافِضَةٌ رَّافِعَةٌ	أَن رَّءَا بُرْهَانَ

● Read the words that include **Idghaam**.
  E.g. جَنَّىٰٓ لَّهُم   نُوحٍ رَّبِّ   أَفِن لَّكُم

● Spell the words which include a **Idghaam**

Step		
Step 1	Alif, Fa, Dhammah = Uf	أُفٍ
Step 2	Fa, Laam, Kasra-tayn = Fil	فٍلٍّ
Step 3	Join the two, = Uf-Fil	أُفٍلٍّ
Step 4	Laam, Fat-hah = La	لَّ
Step 5	Join all previous, = Uf-Fil-La	أُفٍلَّ
Step 6	Kaaf, Meem, Dhammah = Koom	كُمْ
Step 7	Read the entire word, = Uf-Fil-La-Koom	أُفٍلَّكُمْ

If after an empty Noon or Tanween the letters ل or ر appear there will be Idghaam without Ghunnah

Idghaam without Ghunnah only happens when joining on to the letters 'Laam' ل and 'Ra' ر .

Note: Tanween will look like this ـٍـٌـً when Idghaam happens.
Noon will be missing it's Sukoon نْ when Idghaam happens.

  ● I can **read and spell** the words that include **Idghaam** fluently.

  ● I can read each line **fluently in one breath** (without hesitation or pausing).

  ● I can implement all the lessons learnt previously into this exercise.

LESSON 32: IDGHAAM WITH GHUNNAH

أَن نَّطْمِسَ	لَن نَّبْرَحَ	مِن نَّفَادٍ	وَمَن نُّعَمِّرْهُ
مِن نَّذِيرٍ	مِن نُّطْفَةٍ	أَن نَّذِلَّ	مِن نَّبَاتٍ
حَظًّا مِّمَّا	عَدْلٍ مِّنكُمْ	سِحْرٌ مُّبِينٌ	كِتَٰبًا مَّوْقُوتًا
نَبَإٍ مُّسْتَقَرٌّ	سُلْطَٰنًا مُّبِينًا	نَعِيمٌ مُّقِيمٌ	عَذَابًا مُّهِينًا
كُلٌّ يَجْرِى	أَن يُّكَذِّبُونَ	رَجُلٌ يُّرِيدُ	أَن يُّوقِعَ
شَأْنٌ يُّغْنِيهِ	مَن يُّؤْمِنُ	رِدْءًا يُّصَدِّقُنِي	مُنقَلَبٍ يَّنقَلِبُونَ
جَنَّٰتٍ وَّنَهَرٍ	مِن وَّرَثَتِ	سُجَّدًا وَّقِيَٰمًا	يَوْمَئِذٍ وَّاجِفَةٌ
سِرًّا وَّعَلَانِيَةً	زَجْرَةٌ وَّاحِدَةٌ	وَفَٰكِهَةً وَّأَبًّا	ءَامِنًا وَّاجْنُبْنِي

STEP BY STEP

→ Read the words that include **Idghaam**

E.g. جَنَّاتٍ وَنَهَرٍ   كُلٌّ يَجْرِي   حِفْظَانًا   أَن نَطْمِسَ

→ Spell the words which include a **Idghaam**. E.g.

Step 1	Alif, Noon, Fat-hah = An	أَنْ
Step 2	Noon, Taa, Fat-hah = Nat	نَطْ
Step 3	Join the two, An-Nat	أَن نَطْ
Step 4	Meem, Kasrah = Me	مِ
Step 5	Join all previous, An-Nat-Me	أَن نَطْمِ
Step 6	Seen, Fat-hah = Sa	سَ
Step 7	Read the entire word, An-Nat-Me-Sa	أَن نَطْمِسَ

If after an empty Noon or Tanween the letters و م ن ي appear there will be Idghaam with Ghunnah

QUICK TIPS

→ Remember this one word **Yarmaloon**, it has all the letters of Idghaam ي ر م ل و ن, which should help you remember them. **Ya-r-m-l-oo-n** = يَرْمَلُونَ

→ Remember this one word **Yanmoo**, it has all the letters of Idghaam with Ghunnah ي ن م و, it should help you remember them. **Yanmoo** = يَنْمُو

CHECKLIST

✓ I can **read and spell** the words that include **Idghaam** fluently.

✓ I can read each line **fluently in one breath** (without hesitation or pausing).

✓ I can implement all the lessons learnt previously into this exercise.

GRADE 15

The Prophet ﷺ said:

"Read the Qur'aan regularly. By the One in Whose Hand Muhammad's soul is, it escapes from memory faster than a camel does from its tying ropes."

(Muslim)

OVERVIEW

| LESSON 33 | > | IKHFAA | |

Ikhfaa is to stretch with a light nasal sound

- If after an **empty Noon** or **Tanween** any of the following **15 letters** appear: ك ق ف ظ ط ض ص ش س ز ذ د ج ث ت the sound of the **empty Noon** or **Tanween** will be stretched in the nose similar to Ghunnah أَنْتُمْ .
- The difference between the two sounds is that in Ghunnah the tongue is flat when touching the upper palate (roof of the mouth) which makes a deep nasal sound. In Ikhfaa the tip of the tongue touches the upper palate which makes a lighter sound from the nose.

| LESSON 34 | > | IKHFAA MEEM | |

Ikhfaa Meem is to stretch with a deep nasal sound

- If after an **empty Meem** the letter **Ba** ب or **Meem** appears, there will be Ikhfaa مِنْهُم بَطْشًا لَهُم مَغْفِرَةٌ . If any other letter appears then the empty Meem will be read without Ikhfaa.

| LESSON 35 | > | IQLAAB | |

Iqlaab is to replace the empty Noon with a small Meem

- If after: 1. **Empty Noon** or 2. **Fat-hah, Kasrah** or **Dhammah**, the letter **Ba** ب appears, the **empty Noon** will be replaced by a **small Meem** ذَنْۢب .
- However, the **Fat-hah, Kasrah, Dhammah,** will join straight onto the small Meem and will be read with a Ghunnah أَبَدًاۢبِمَا .

| LESSON 36 | > | NOON QUTNI | |

Noon Qutni is to add a Noon with a Kasrah and to replace a Tanween with a single Harakah ٍ = ِ

- If after a **Tanween** a **Saakin** letter appears 1. Tanween changes to single Harakah 2. If there are any Alifs they will be cancelled 3. Add a Noon Kasrah before the Saakin letter (& join) نُوحٌ ابْنَهُ = نُوحُ ابْنَهُ .

LESSON 33 — IKHFAA

أَنْتُم

تُنذِرُ	مِنكُم	جُنِدٍ	أَنتُم
مُنقَلَبٍ	أَنجَـكُم	تَنشَقُّ	أَنفَقُوا
يَنطِقُونَ	يَحْزُنكَ	مَنشُورًا	فَٱنطَلَقَا
يَنظُرُونَ	أَنشَأْنَهُ	أَنفُسَهُم	نَنقُصُهَا
ذُرِّيَّةً ضِعَافًا	ثَمَنًا قَلِيلًا	مِن قَبْلُ	يَنصُرُونَهُ
مِمَّن تَرْضَوْنَ	عَذَابًا شَدِيدًا	رِجَالًا كَثِيرًا	أَذًى كَثِيرًا
خَالِدِافِيهَا	مِن قَبْلِكُم	لَن تُقَاتِلُوا	مِن فَضْلِهِ
وَأَنفُسَنَاوَأَنفُسَكُم	أَوْ قُتِلَ ٱنقَلَبْتُم	سُورَةٌ تُنَبِّئُهُم	مَرْجُوًّاقَبْلَ

STEP BY STEP

- Read the words that include Ikhfaa. E.g. Annn-tum أَنْتُمْ , Junnn-din جُنِدٍ , Minnn-kum مِنْكُمْ.

- Spell the words that include Ikhfaa (refer to Lesson 06: Sukoon).

- Identify and apply Ikhfaa properly.

If after an empty Noon or Tanween any of these fifteen letters appear ت ث ج د ذ ز س ش ص ض ط ظ ف ق ك there will be a stretch with a light nasal sound.

QUICK TIPS

There are 2 ways to learn the Ikhfaa letters:
1) By elimination: After excluding the Ba, Izhaar & Idghaam letters, you are left with the Ikhfaa letters. OR
2) Memorising: Memorise the Ikhfaa letters and try to say them under 5 seconds.

Note: Tanween will look like this ـً ـٍ ـٌ when Idghaam or Ikhfaa happens.
Noon will be missing it's Sukoon ن when Idghaam or Ikhfaa happens.

CHECKLIST

- I can **read and spell** the words that include Ikhfaa.

- I can read each line **fluently in one breath** (without hesitation or pausing).

- I can implement all the lessons learnt previously into this exercise.

Comments

LESSON 34: IKHFAA MEEM

هُم بَطْ

فَهُم مُّسْلِمُونَ	سَبَقَكُم بِهَا	لَهُم مَغْفِرَةٌ	مِنْهُم بَطْشًا
أَمْوَالِهِم	أَتْمَمْتَ	تَمْشِى	نَمْلَةٌ
وَهُم مُّهْتَدُونَ	بِهِم مُّؤْمِنُونَ	بَعْضُكُم بَعْضًا	لَهُمْ قَوْلًا
أَنتُم مُّطَّلِعُونَ	أَخَاهُمْ صَالِحًا	يَأْتِيكُم بِلَيْلٍ	لَكُمْ فَتْحٌ
أَنتُم بِمُعْجِزِينَ	فَأَمْسِكُوهُنَّ	أَعْمَالَهُمْ فِيهَا	وَمِثْلَهُم مَّعَهُمْ
كُنتُم مُّجْرِمِينَ	فَهُم مُّقْمَحُونَ	لَهُمْ لَا تَعْدُوا	أَذَاقَهُم مِّنْهُ
وَاضْمُمْ إِلَيْكَ	مِنْهُم مُّقْتَصِدٌ	لَمْ يُفَرِّقُوا	فَهُمْ يُوزَعُونَ
فَلَكُمْ رُءُوسُ	أَصَبْتُم مِّثْلَيْهَا	دَخَلْتُم بِهِنَّ	كُنتُم مَّرْضَىٰ

- Read the words that include Ikhfaa and Izhaar.
  E.g. Ikhfaa: Minhummm-batshan مِنْهُم بَطْشًا ,
  Izhaar: Namlatun نَمْلَةٌ ,

- Spell the words that include Ikhfaa and Izhaar.
  (refer to Lesson 06: Sukoon)

If after an empty Meem مْ the letters ب or مْ appear then there will be a stretch on the empty Meem with a deep nasal sound.

The only 2 letters to remember after the empty Meem are: **Ba and Meem.**
Note: Meem will be missing it's Sukoon ْ when Ikhfaa happens.

- I can **read and spell** the words that include **Ikhfaa** and **Izhaar** fluently.
- I can read each line **fluently in one breath** (without hesitation or pausing).
- I can implement all the lessons learnt previously into this exercise.

LESSON 35 — IQLAAB

ذَنْبٌ

يَنْبَغِي	فَٱنْبِذْ	أَنْبَاءِ	ذَنْبٍ
زَوْجٍ بَهِيجٍ	وَاقِعٌ بِهِمْ	عَلِيمٌ بِهِ	أَبَدًا بِمَا
مَنْ بَخِلَ	مِنْ بَابٍ	لَيُنْبَذَنَّ	مِنْ بَيْنِ
مَكَانٍ بَعِيدٍ	جُدَدٌ بِيضٌ	بِٱلْجَنْبِ	سُنْبُلَاتٍ
بِثَمَنٍ بَخْسٍ	وَضَائِقٌ بِهِ	سَوَاءٌ بَيْنَنَا	مُنْفَطِرٌ بِهِ
سَيِّئَةٍ بِمِثْلِهَا	سُلْطَانٍ بِهَذَا	قَرْيَةٍ بَطِرَتْ	كُلًّا بِسِيمَاهُمْ
لَيًّا بِأَلْسِنَتِهِمْ	قَآئِمًۢا بِٱلْقِسْطِ	مُصَدِّقًا بِكَلِمَةٍ	بَصِيرٌ بِٱلْعِبَادِ
ءَاخِذٌ بِنَاصِيَتِهَا	أَوْدِيَةٌ بِقَدَرِهَا	مُؤَذِّنٌ بَيْنَهُمْ	وَيَسْتَنْبِئُونَكَ

- Read the words that include Iqlaab.
  E.g. Thamm-bin ذَنْبٍ , Ammbaaaaa-e أَنْبَآءٍ , Famm-bith فَأَنْبِذْ .

- Spell the words which include Iqlaab.
  E.g.

Step 1	Thaal, Meem, Fat-hah = Tham	ذَمَ
Step 2	Ba, Kasrah-tayn = Bin	بٍ
Step 3	Read the entire word, Tham-Bin	ذَنْبٍ

If after: 1. Empty Noon or
2. Fat-hah, Kasrah or Dhammah, the letter Ba ب appears, the empty Noon will be replaced with a small Meem م and will be read with a deep nasal sound similar to Ghunnah.

When joining onto the small Meem always make a stretched nasal sound.

Note: **Tanween** will look like this when Idghaam or Ikhfaa happens.
Noon will be missing it's Sukoon ن when Idghaam, Ikhfaa or Iqlaab happens.

- I can **read and spell** the words that include **Iqlaab** fluently.

- I can read each line **fluently in one breath** (without hesitation or pausing.)

- I can implement all the lessons learnt previously into this exercise.

LESSON 36: NOON QUTNI

حُ اْبْ

خَيْرًا ٱلْوَصِيَّةُ	قَدِيرٌ ٱلَّذِى	عَادًا ٱلْأُولَى	نُوحٌ ٱبْنَهُ
لَهْوًا ٱنفَضُّوا	شِيبًا ٱلسَّمَآءُ	لُمَزَةٍ ٱلَّذِى	نَذِيرًا ٱلَّذِى
جَمِيعًا ٱلَّذِى	فَخُورٍ ٱلَّذِينَ	رَجُلٌ ٱفْتَرَى	خَبِيرًا ٱلَّذِى
شَكُورٌ ٱلَّذِى	مُرْتَابٌ ٱلَّذِينَ	يَوْمَئِذٍ ٱلْحَقُّ	إِفْكٌ ٱفْتَرَاهُ
يَوْمَئِذٍ ٱلْمُسْتَقَرُّ	عَادٌ ٱلْمُرْسَلِينَ	بِزِينَةٍ ٱلْكَوَاكِبِ	نُفُورًا ٱسْتِكْبَارًا
نُوحٌ ٱلْمُرْسَلِينَ	شَيْئًا ٱلتَّخَذَهَا	لُوطٍ ٱلْمُرْسَلِينَ	مَقْدُورًا ٱلَّذِينَ
مَثَلًا ٱلْقَوْمُ ٱلَّذِينَ	وَأَمْوَالٌ ٱقْتَرَفْتُمُوهَا	وَرَهْبَانِيَّةً ٱبْتَدَعُوهَا
جَنَّاتِ عَدْنٍ ٱلَّتِى	إِلَى بَعْضِ ٱلْقَوْلَ	قَوْمًا ٱللَّهُ مُهْلِكُهُمْ

STEP BY STEP

- ▸ Read the words that include a Noon Qutni without spelling. E.g. Noo-hu-nib-na-hoo نُوحٌ ٱبْنَهُ, Aa-da-nil-oolaa عَادًا ٱلْأُولَىٰ .

- ▸ Spell the words which include a Noon Qutni. E.g.

Step 1	Noon, Waw, Dhammah = Noo	نُو
Step 2	Ha, Dhammah = Hu	حُ
Step 3	Join the two, Noo-Hu	نُوحُ
Step 4	Noon, Ba, Kasrah = Nib	ٱبْ
Step 5	Join all previous, Noo-Hu-Nib	نُوحُ ٱبْ
Step 6	Noon, Fat-hah = Na	نَ
Step 7	Join all previous, Noo-Hu-Nib-Na	نُوحُ ٱبْنَ
Step 8	Ha, Madd Dhammah = Hoo	هُو
Step 9	Read the entire word, Noo-Hu-Nib-Na-Hoo	نُوحُ ٱبْنَهُ

Add a Noon with a Kasrah and replace the Tanween with a single Harakah.

QUICK TIPS

Add a Noon with a Kasrah between the Tanween and Saakin letter.
Replace the Tanween with a single Harakah.

Single Harakah   Tanween

CHECKLIST

- ✓ I can **read and spell** the words that include a hidden Noon with a Kasrah fluently.

- ✓ I can read each line **fluently in one breath** (without hesitation or pausing).

- ✓ I can implement all the lessons learnt previously into this exercise.

GRADE 16

The Prophet ﷺ said:

"Any group of people that assemble in one of the Houses of Allaah to recite the Book of Allaah, learning and teaching it, tranquility will descend upon them, mercy will engulf them, Angels will surround them and Allaah will make mention of them to those (the angels) in His proximity."

[Muslim]

OVERVIEW

LESSON 37 > **STOPPING ON ROUND TA (TA MARBOOTAH)**

- When stopping on a **Taa Marbootah** ة the Taa will be **replaced** by a **Haa Saakin** هْ regardless of the Harakah on the Taa.

LESSON 38 > **STOPPING ON FAT-HA-TAYN**

- If the last letter has a **Fat-ha-tayn** and an **Alif** e.g. رًا : Fat-ha-tayn will be **replaced** with a **Fat-hah** رَ.
- **Fat-ha-tayn** without an **Alif** after it e.g. عً : Fat-ha-tayn will be **replaced** by a **Fat-hah** followed by an **Alif** عَا.

LESSON 39 > **WAQF (STOPPING)**

- **Nothing changes If**: The last letter is a Saakin letter كُمْ or Fat-hah followed by an Alif هَا or Madd Fat-hah نَى.
- **Shaddah**: If the last letter has a Shaddah on it تِّ, then the Shaddah will remain but the Harakah will be silenced تّْ.
- **Everything else**: (Leaving aside the Taa Marbootah, Fat-ha-tayn and the rules learnt above), if any other Harakah appears on the last letter فَقَتَلَهُ, the Harakah will be replaced by a Sukoon فَقَتَلَهْ.

LESSON 40 > **WAQF (STOPPING)**

- Ensure all previous **Tajweed rules** are exercised in this lesson.

LESSON 41 > **SAKTAH (PAUSE)**

- **Saktah** سْ is to pause the recitation without taking a breath for a second, then continue to read وَقِيلَ مَنْ ۜ رَاقٍ .
- There are four places in the Qur'aan where Saktah is compulsory, they have been coloured in red.

LESSON 37: STOPPING ON 'TAA' MARBOOTAH

مَثَلُ ٱلْجَنَّةِ ۝	كُتُبٌ قَيِّمَةٌ ۝	مِنْهُم تُقَىٰةً ۝
وَفَاكِهَةٍ كَثِيرَةٍ ۝	وَأَقِمِ ٱلصَّلَوٰةَ ۝	ذُرِّيَّةً طَيِّبَةً ۝
تَحْتَ ٱلشَّجَرَةِ ۝	حَيَوٰةً طَيِّبَةً ۝	أَهْلِ ٱلْمَدِينَةِ ۝
وَهُدًى وَرَحْمَةٌ ۝	سُورَةٌ مُّحْكَمَةٌ ۝	أَم بِهِۦ جِنَّةٌ ۝
كَمَا لَهُمْ ءَالِهَةٌ ۝	وَمَغَانِمَ كَثِيرَةً ۝	فِى جَنَّةٍ عَالِيَةٍ ۝
إِذَا دَعَاكُمْ دَعْوَةً ۝	أَصْحَابَ ٱلْقَرْيَةِ ۝	ٱلْأَرْضُ ٱلْمَيْتَةُ ۝
وُجُوهُهُم مُّسْوَدَّةٌ ۝	ظَاهِرَةً وَبَاطِنَةً ۝	أَعِظُكُم بِوَاحِدَةٍ ۝
وَتُسَبِّحُوهُ بُكْرَةً ۝	فِى قُلُوبِهِمُ ٱلْحَمِيَّةَ ۝	ضَاحِكَةٌ مُّسْتَبْشِرَةٌ ۝

   Completed on

STEP BY STEP

▸ Apply Waqf correctly on words that end with the **round Taa** (Taa Marbootah).

Before Waqf	After Waqf
مَثَلُ ٱلْجَنَّةِ ۞	مَثَلُ ٱلْجَنَّهْ ۞
كُتُبٌ قَيِّمَةٌ ۞	كُتُبٌ قَيِّمَهْ ۞
مِنْهُم ثَقَلَةٌ ۞	مِنْهُم ثَقَلَهْ ۞

QUICK TIPS

When stopping on a **Round Taa** ة , it will always be replaced with a **Haa** ه **Saakin**.

CHECKLIST

- I can read and apply Waqf on **Taa Marbootah** fluently.
- I can read each line **fluently and quickly**.
- I can implement all the lessons learnt previously into this exercise.

LESSON 38: STOPPING ON FAT-HA-TAYN

خِطْأً كَبِيرًا ۞	رَبِّ رَضِيًّا ۞	بَشَرًا رَّسُولًا ۞
بُكْرَةً وَّعَشِيًّا ۞	صَعِيدًا زَلَقًا ۞	سُجَّدًا وَّبُكِيًّا ۞
مَكَانًا عَلِيًّا ۞	رَسُولًا نَّبِيًّا ۞	بَيْنَكُمْ شَهِيدًا ۞
أَقْرَبَ رُحْمًا ۞	وَلِيًّا مُّرْشِدًا ۞	وَكَبِّرْهُ تَكْبِيرًا ۞
رُطَبًا جَنِيًّا ۞	تَحْتَكِ سَرِيًّا ۞	أُبْعَثُ حَيًّا ۞
صِرَاطًا سَوِيًّا ۞	مَكَانًا شَرْقِيًّا ۞	غُلَامًا زَكِيًّا ۞
إِلَىٰ أَجَلٍ مُّسَمًّى ۞	وَنَزَّلْنَاهُ تَنْزِيلًا ۞	يُحْسِنُونَ صُنْعًا ۞
وَأَضْعَفُ جُنْدًا ۞	وَازْدَادُوا تِسْعًا ۞	أَوْ أَمْضِيَ حُقُبًا ۞

▸▸ Read and apply the Waqf on Fat-ha-tayn correctly. E.g.

Before Waqf	After Waqf
خِطْأً كَبِيرًا ۞	خِطْأً كَبِيرًا ۞
رَبِّ رَضِيًّا ۞	رَبِّ رَضِيًّا ۞
بَشَرًا رَّسُولًا ۞	بَشَرًا رَّسُولًا ۞

When stopping on a Fat-ha-tayn عًا remove one Fat-hah. You should be left with a Fat-hah followed by an Alif عَا .

- I can apply **Waqf on Fat-ha-tayn** fluently.
- I can read **each line fluently** (without hesitation or pausing).
- I can implement all the lessons learnt previously into this exercise.

Comments

Lesson 39 — WAQF

وَأَوْفُواْ بِٱلْعَهْدِ ۝	رُدُّوهَا عَلَىٰ ۝	أَغْنَىٰ وَأَقْنَىٰ ۝
أَسْمِعْ بِهِمْ ۝	عَلَّمَ ٱلْقُرْءَانَ ۝	رَبُّ ٱلْمَشْرِقَيْنِ ۝
ذَٰلِكَ وَأَصْلَحُواْ ۝	كَذِبًا أَمْ بِهِۦ ۝	وَرَفَعْنَا لَكَ ذِكْرَكَ ۝
رَبِّي أَكْرَمَنِ ۝	فَقَالَ أَكْفِلْنِيهَا ۝	غُلَامًا فَقَتَلَهُۥ ۝
وَأَدْبَارَ ٱلسُّجُودِ ۝	وَنَـَٔا بِجَانِبِهِۦ ۝	وَبَرًّۢا بِوَالِدَتِي ۝
ءَاتَيْتُهُنَّ كُلُّهُنَّ ۝	هَاجَرْنَ مَعَكَ ۝	وَحْيٌ يُوحَىٰ ۝
شَاكِرًا لِّأَنْعُمِهِۦ ۝	خَشْيَةَ ٱلْإِنفَاقِ ۝	وَتَرَبَّصْتُمْ وَٱرْتَبْتُمْ ۝
قِسْمَةٌ ضِيزَىٰ ۝	قِيلَ ٱرْجِعُواْ وَرَآءَكُمْ ۝	ٱقْرَأْ وَرَبُّكَ ٱلْأَكْرَمُ ۝

STEP BY STEP

▸ Apply Waqf correctly. E.g.

Before Waqf	After Waqf
وَأَوْفُواْ بِٱلْعَهْدِ ۞	وَأَوْفُواْ بِٱلْعَهْدْ ۞
رُدُّوهَا عَلَىٰ ۞	رُدُّوهَا عَلَىٰ ۞
أَغْنَىٰ وَأَقْنَىٰ ۞	أَغْنَىٰ وَأَقْنَىٰ ۞

When applying Waqf the last letter will be given a Sukoon unless some of the following appear on the last letter: Ta Marbootah ةٍ , Fat-hah-tayn اً , Madd Fathah ىٰ , Fat-hah followed by an Alif هَا , Shaddah عَلَّ .

QUICK TIPS

Does change

	=	
ةْ	=	هْ
رَا	=	رًا
ىْ	=	ىّ
فَقَتَلَهْ	=	فَقَتَلَهُ

Does not change

	=	
كُمْ	=	كُمْ
هَا	=	هَا
نَىٰ	=	نَىٰ

CHECKLIST

- ✓ I can **read and spell** the words that include **Waqf** fluently.
- ✓ I can read and apply **Waqf** correctly.
- ✓ I can implement all the lessons learnt previously into this exercise.

LESSON 40: WAQF ON THREE WORDS

إِلَٰهُكُمْ إِلَٰهٌ وَاحِدٌ ۝	أَنِ ٱعْبُدُوا۟ ٱللَّهَ ۝	أَءِلَٰهٌ مَّعَ ٱللَّهِ ۝
عَلَّمَهُۥ شَدِيدُ ٱلْقُوَىٰ ۝	ثُمَّ أَدْبَرَ وَٱسْتَكْبَرَ ۝	نُورٌ عَلَىٰ نُورٍ ۝
وَٱللَّهُ وَاسِعٌ عَلِيمٌ ۝	أَفَغَيْرَ ٱللَّهِ تَتَّقُونَ ۝	قُمِ ٱلَّيْلَ إِلَّا قَلِيلًا ۝
وَتَسِيرُ ٱلْجِبَالُ سَيْرًا ۝	لَّا يَمَسُّهُۥ إِلَّا ٱلْمُطَهَّرُونَ ۝	وَكُنتُمْ أَزْوَٰجًا ثَلَٰثَةً ۝
وَلَنِعْمَ دَارُ ٱلْمُتَّقِينَ ۝	فَشَٰرِبُونَ شُرْبَ ٱلْهِيمِ ۝	عِندَ سِدْرَةِ ٱلْمُنتَهَىٰ ۝
وَلَأَجْرُ ٱلْءَاخِرَةِ أَكْبَرُ ۝	يَخْلُقُ ٱللَّهُ مَا يَشَآءُ ۝	أَفَتُمَٰرُونَهُۥ عَلَىٰ مَا يَرَىٰ ۝
إِنِّى أَنَا ٱلنَّذِيرُ ٱلْمُبِينُ ۝	وَجَعَلَ ٱلشَّمْسَ سِرَاجًا ۝	إِذَا رُجَّتِ ٱلْأَرْضُ رَجًّا ۝
فَلَآ أُقْسِمُ بِمَوَٰقِعِ ٱلنُّجُومِ ۝	قِيلَ لَهَا ٱدْخُلِى ٱلصَّرْحَ ۝	كَأَنَّهُمْ حُمُرٌ مُّسْتَنفِرَةٌ ۝

   Completed on   /   /

STEP BY STEP

→ Apply Waqf correctly. E.g.

Before Waqf	After Waqf
ءَإِلَٰهٌ مَّعَ ٱللَّهِ ۝	ءَإِلَٰهٌ مَّعَ ٱللَّهْ ۝
أَنِ اعْبُدُواْ ٱللَّهَ ۝	أَنِ اعْبُدُواْ ٱللَّهْ ۝
إِلَٰهُكُمْ إِلَٰهٌ وَّاحِدٌ ۝	إِلَٰهُكُمْ إِلَٰهٌ وَّاحِدْ ۝

When applying Waqf the last letter will be given a Sukoon unless some of the following appear on the last letter: Ta Marbootah ةٍ , Fat-hah-tayn اً , Madd Fathah نَىٰ , Fat-hah followed by an Alif هَا , Shaddah عَلَيَّ .

QUICK TIPS

Does change			Does not change		
ةْ	=	ةٌ	كُمْ	=	كُمْ
رَا	=	رًا	هَا	=	هَا
نَىٰ	=	نَىٰ	نَىٰ	=	نَىٰ
فَقَتَلَهْ	=	فَقَتَلَهُۥ			

CHECKLIST

- ✓ I can **read and spell** the words that include **Waqf** fluently.
- ✓ I can read and apply **Waqf** correctly.
- ✓ I can implement all the lessons learnt previously into this exercise.

Comments

LESSON 41 — SAKTAH

مَنْ رَاقٍ

كَلَّا بَلْ رَانَ عَلَىٰ قُلُوبِهِم مَّا كَانُوا۟ يَكْسِبُونَ

كَلَّا إِذَا بَلَغَتِ ٱلتَّرَاقِيَ ۝ وَقِيلَ مَنْ رَاقٍ

وَلَمْ يَجْعَل لَّهُۥ عِوَجَا ۜ قَيِّمًا لِّيُنذِرَ بَأْسًا شَدِيدًا مِّن لَّدُنْهُ وَيُبَشِّرَ ٱلْمُؤْمِنِينَ

قَالُوا۟ يَـٰوَيْلَنَا مَنۢ بَعَثَنَا مِن مَّرْقَدِنَا ۜ هَـٰذَا مَا وَعَدَ ٱلرَّحْمَـٰنُ وَصَدَقَ ٱلْمُرْسَلُونَ

→ Read the words that include a Saktah without any hesitation. E.g.

كَلَّا بَلْ ۜ رَانَ عَلَىٰ قُلُوبِهِم مَّا كَانُوا يَكْسِبُونَ

كَلَّآ إِذَا بَلَغَتِ ٱلتَّرَاقِىَ وَقِيلَ مَنْ ۜ رَاقٍ

وَلَمْ يَجْعَل لَّهُۥ عِوَجَا ۜ قَيِّمًا لِّيُنذِرَ بَأْسًا شَدِيدًا مِّن لَّدُنْهُ وَيُبَشِّرَ ٱلْمُؤْمِنِينَ

قَالُوا يَٰوَيْلَنَا مَنۢ بَعَثَنَا مِن مَّرْقَدِنَا ۜ هَٰذَا مَا وَعَدَ ٱلرَّحْمَٰنُ وَصَدَقَ ٱلْمُرْسَلُونَ

You pause without taking a breath and then continue. It's like a comma in English.

- ◉ I can **read and spell** the words that include **Saktah** fluently.
- ◉ I can read each part **in one breath** and applying **Saktah** correctly.
- ◉ I can implement all the lessons learnt previously into this exercise.

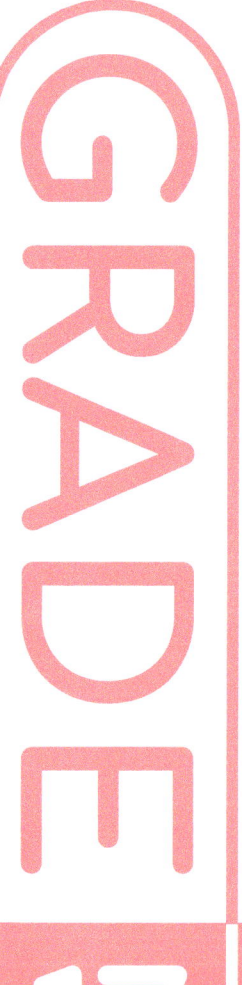

GRADE 17

The Prophet ﷺ said:

"The best amongst you is he who learns the Qur'an and teaches it to others."

(Bukhaari)

OVERVIEW

LESSON 42 > ADVANCE STOPPING AND SAJDAH

- This symbol will always come in pairs in a verse, you must **stop at one** and **carry on** at the other. The choice is yours. Do not stop at both.
- When a line comes above a word you must do a Sajdah Tilaawah at the end of that verse (Ayah).

Note: *This line* وَٱسْجُدْ *indicates where the Sajdah is and this word* السجدة *at the end of the verse (Ayah) indicates that Sajdah needs to be done.*

LESSON 43 > HUROOF AL-MUQATTA'AAT

- Here we read the letter rather than the sound and stretch it according to the symbol on top of it. These letters are an exception to the general rule.
  For example: Nooooon نٓ , Qaaaaaf قٓ .
- By this stage the student should be familiar with all the **Waqf rules** and previous lessons.

LESSON 44 > WAQF (STOPPING)

- When you read the longer verses and run out of breath, wherever you stop mid sentence, you will still need to apply the waqf rule.
  Then simply resume the recitation from one or two words before where the Waqf was applied.
- By this stage the student should be familiar with all the Spellings, Tajweed and Waqf rules.

Symbol	Meaning
ۘ	Should stop
مـ	Must stop
لا	Can't stop
ج	Optional (stop or continue)
ص	Can stop but better to continue
ق	Can continue but better to stop

LESSON 42: ADVANCE STOPPING AND SAJDAH

ذَٰلِكَ ٱلْكِتَٰبُ لَا رَيْبَ ۛ فِيهِ ۛ هُدًى لِّلْمُتَّقِينَ ۝

سجدة — كَلَّا لَا تُطِعْهُ وَٱسْجُدْ وَٱقْتَرِب ۩ ۝

سجدة — وَإِذَا قُرِئَ عَلَيْهِمُ ٱلْقُرْءَانُ لَا يَسْجُدُونَ ۩ ۝

إِنَّمَا يُؤْمِنُ بِـَٔايَٰتِنَا ٱلَّذِينَ إِذَا ذُكِّرُوا۟ بِهَا خَرُّوا۟ سُجَّدًا

سجدة — وَسَبَّحُوا۟ بِحَمْدِ رَبِّهِمْ وَهُمْ لَا يَسْتَكْبِرُونَ ۩ ۝

STEP BY STEP

•▶ Read and learn the Aayaat (sentences) that include **advance Waqf and Sajdah** properly.

ۛ	Should stop
م	Must stop
لا	Can't stop
ج	Optional (stop or continue)
صلى	Can stop but better to continue
قلى	Can continue but better to stop

QUICK TIPS

•▶ ۛ = Stop at one and carry on at the other.

•▶ وَٱسْجُدْ = Sajdah is compulsory after this is read.

•▶ 🕌 = Sajdah should be done now or can be done.

CHECKLIST

✓ I can apply **advance Waqf and Sajdah** properly.

✓ I can read each part in **one breath** correctly.

✓ I can implement all the lessons learnt previously into this exercise.

LESSON 43: HUROOF AL-MUQATTA'AAT

يٰسٓ

قٓ	نٓ	صٓ	طه
يسٓ	حمٓ	طسٓ	الٓمٓرٰ
طسٓمٓ	عٓسٓقٓ	الٓمٓصٓ	كهيعصٓ

COMPLETE VERSE FLUENCY

حمٓ ۞ عٓسٓقٓ ۞ كَذَٰلِكَ يُوحِىٓ إِلَيْكَ وَإِلَى ٱلَّذِينَ مِن قَبْلِكَ ٱللَّهُ ٱلْعَزِيزُ ٱلْحَكِيمُ ۞ الٓمٓرٰ تِلْكَ ءَايَٰتُ ٱلْكِتَٰبِ ۞ كهيعصٓ ۞ ذِكْرُ رَحْمَتِ رَبِّكَ عَبْدَهُۥ زَكَرِيَّآ ۞ يسٓ ۞ وَٱلْقُرْءَانِ ٱلْحَكِيمِ ۞ حمٓ ۞ تَنزِيلٌ مِّنَ ٱلرَّحْمَٰنِ ٱلرَّحِيمِ ۞ كِتَٰبٌ فُصِّلَتْ ءَايَٰتُهُۥ قُرْءَانًا عَرَبِيًّا لِّقَوْمٍ يَعْلَمُونَ ۞ وَلَا تَحْسَبَنَّ ٱلَّذِينَ قُتِلُوا۟ فِى سَبِيلِ ٱللَّهِ أَمْوَٰتًۢا بَلْ أَحْيَآءٌ عِندَ رَبِّهِمْ يُرْزَقُونَ ۞ الٓرٰ تِلْكَ ءَايَٰتُ ٱلْكِتَٰبِ ٱلْحَكِيمِ ۞

Completed on   /   /

- Read the **Haroof Al-Muqatta'aat** correctly. E.g. "Qaaaaaf" قٓ , "Nooooon" نٓ , "Saaaaad" صٓ .

- Spell the Haroof Al-Muqatta'aat. E.g.

 Step 1   Qaaf-Madd "Qaaaaaf"

- Identify the Haroof Al-Muqatta'aat. They only come at the beginning of certain Surahs.

- You only say the letters and then stretch them depending on the type of Madd.

- ✓ I can **read and spell** the Haroof Al-Muqatta'aat.
- ✓ I can read each line **fluently and quickly**.
- ✓ I can implement all the lessons learnt previously into this exercise.

LESSON 44: COMPLETE VERSE FLUENCY

وَقُلِ ٱلْحَقُّ مِن رَّبِّكُمْ ۖ فَمَن شَآءَ فَلْيُؤْمِن وَمَن شَآءَ فَلْيَكْفُرْ إِنَّآ أَعْتَدْنَا لِلظَّٰلِمِينَ نَارًا أَحَاطَ بِهِمْ سُرَادِقُهَا ۚ وَإِن يَسْتَغِيثُوا۟ يُغَاثُوا۟ بِمَآءٍ كَٱلْمُهْلِ يَشْوِى ٱلْوُجُوهَ ۚ بِئْسَ ٱلشَّرَابُ وَسَآءَتْ مُرْتَفَقًا ۞ يَٰزَكَرِيَّآ إِنَّا نُبَشِّرُكَ بِغُلَٰمٍ ٱسْمُهُۥ يَحْيَىٰ لَمْ نَجْعَل لَّهُۥ مِن قَبْلُ سَمِيًّا ۞ يَٰيَحْيَىٰ خُذِ ٱلْكِتَٰبَ بِقُوَّةٍ ۖ وَءَاتَيْنَٰهُ ٱلْحُكْمَ صَبِيًّا ۞ وَٱذْكُرْ فِى ٱلْكِتَٰبِ مَرْيَمَ إِذِ ٱنتَبَذَتْ مِنْ أَهْلِهَا مَكَانًا شَرْقِيًّا ۞ قَالَ كَذَٰلِكِ قَالَ رَبُّكِ هُوَ عَلَىَّ هَيِّنٌ ۖ وَلِنَجْعَلَهُۥٓ ءَايَةً لِّلنَّاسِ وَرَحْمَةً مِّنَّا ۚ وَكَانَ أَمْرًا مَّقْضِيًّا ۞ هَلْ أَتَىٰكَ حَدِيثُ ضَيْفِ إِبْرَٰهِيمَ ٱلْمُكْرَمِينَ ۞ وَهَلْ أَتَىٰكَ نَبَؤُا۟ ٱلْخَصْمِ إِذْ تَسَوَّرُوا۟ ٱلْمِحْرَابَ ۞

Completed on   /   /

STEP BY STEP

- Identify and apply all the Tajweed rules from Grade 12 onwards properly.
- Identify and apply Waqf properly.

ۘ	Should stop
م	Must stop
لا	Can't stop
ج	Optional (stop or continue)
ص	Can stop but better to continue
قلى	Can continue but better to stop

QUICK TIPS

- Read at a medium pace without stretching Fat-hah, Kasrah and Dhammah.
- When you come across an empty Noon or Tanween lookout for a Tajweed rule.

CHECKLIST

- I can **read with Tajweed** by myself.
- I can read each Ayah (verse) fluently in one breath.
- I can read the entire Qaa'idah before progressing onto the Qur'aan.

LESSON 44: COMPLETE VERSE FLUENCY

قَدْ صَدَّقْتَ ٱلرُّءْيَآ ۚ إِنَّا كَذَٰلِكَ نَجْزِى ٱلْمُحْسِنِينَ ۞ إِنَّهُمْ كَانُوا۟

إِذَا قِيلَ لَهُمْ لَآ إِلَٰهَ إِلَّا ٱللَّهُ يَسْتَكْبِرُونَ ۞ فَفِرُّوٓا۟ إِلَى ٱللَّهِ ۖ

إِنِّى لَكُم مِّنْهُ نَذِيرٌ مُّبِينٌ ۞ ٱللَّهُ لَآ إِلَٰهَ إِلَّا هُوَ ۖ لَهُ ٱلْأَسْمَآءُ ٱلْحُسْنَىٰ

وَهَلْ أَتَىٰكَ حَدِيثُ مُوسَىٰٓ ۞ أَتَوَاصَوْا۟ بِهِۦ ۚ بَلْ هُمْ قَوْمٌ طَاغُونَ ۞

أَمْ خَلَقُوا۟ ٱلسَّمَٰوَٰتِ وَٱلْأَرْضَ ۚ بَل لَّا يُوقِنُونَ ۞ سَخَّرَهَا عَلَيْهِمْ

سَبْعَ لَيَالٍ وَثَمَٰنِيَةَ أَيَّامٍ حُسُومًا ۖ فَتَرَى ٱلْقَوْمَ فِيهَا صَرْعَىٰ

كَأَنَّهُمْ أَعْجَازُ نَخْلٍ خَاوِيَةٍ ۞ وَلَهُۥ مَن فِى ٱلسَّمَٰوَٰتِ وَٱلْأَرْضِ ۚ

قُلْ لَّهُۥ قَٰنِتُونَ ۞ قُلُوبٌ يَوْمَئِذٍ وَاجِفَةٌ ۞ أَبْصَٰرُهَا خَٰشِعَةٌ ۞

أَمْ حَسِبْتَ أَنَّ أَصْحَٰبَ ٱلْكَهْفِ وَٱلرَّقِيمِ كَانُوا۟ مِنْ ءَايَٰتِنَا عَجَبًا ۞

STEP BY STEP

•▶ Apply the following correctly:

- ▶ Qalqalah
- ▶ Ghunnah
- ▶ Izhaar
- ▶ Ra rule
- ▶ Word of Allaah rule
- ▶ Idghaam
- ▶ Ikhfaa
- ▶ Meem Saakin
- ▶ Iqlaab
- ▶ Noon Qutni
- ▶ Saktah and Waqfah
- ▶ Waqf on "Ta" Marbootah
- ▶ Waqf on Fat-ha-tayn
- ▶ Waqf

QUICK TIPS

If an Alif with a small Saad ٱ comes at the beginning of an Ayah (verse) or word then:
1. Read it with a Fat-hah if a Laam is coming after it or,
2. Read it with a Kasrah if the third letter has a Fat-hah or Kasrah or,
3. Read it with a Dhammah if the third letter has a Dhammah on it.

CHECKLIST

- ⓘ I can **read with Tajweed** by myself.
- ⓘ I can read each Ayah (verse) **fluently in one breath** (without hesitation or pausing).
- ⓘ I can read the entire Qaa'idah before progressing onto the Qur'aan.

Comments

GRADE 18

The Prophet ﷺ said:

"He who does not memorise any part from the Qur'an he is like the ruined house."

(Tirmidhi)

OVERVIEW

LESSON 45 **MEMORISATION OF THE LAST 10 SURAHS**

- Every student must learn the last 10 Surahs from memory with the correct pronunciation ensuring all Tajweed rules are applied properly.
- These Surahs are normally read during prayers as they are short and easy to learn. It is very important to memorise at least a portion of the Qur'aan so that Allaah may shower His mercy upon us.
- If an Alif with a small Saad comes at the beginning of an Ayah (verse) or word then:
    1. Read it with a **Fat-hah if a Laam is coming after it** or,
    2. Read it with a **Kasrah if the third letter has a Fat-hah or Kasrah** or,
    3. Read it with a **Dhammah if the third letter has a Dhammah** on it.

ۆ	Should stop
م	Must stop
لا	Can't stop
ج	Optional (stop or continue)
ص	Can stop but better to continue
قل	Can continue but better to stop

FINAL > **STUDENT CHECKLIST**

- Every student should go through the checklist and be confident in what they have learnt.

LESSON 45: LAST 10 SURAHS

بِسْمِ ٱللَّهِ ٱلرَّحْمَٰنِ ٱلرَّحِيمِ ۝

ٱلْحَمْدُ لِلَّهِ رَبِّ ٱلْعَٰلَمِينَ ۝ ٱلرَّحْمَٰنِ ٱلرَّحِيمِ ۝ مَٰلِكِ يَوْمِ ٱلدِّينِ ۝ إِيَّاكَ نَعْبُدُ وَإِيَّاكَ نَسْتَعِينُ ۝ ٱهْدِنَا ٱلصِّرَٰطَ ٱلْمُسْتَقِيمَ ۝ صِرَٰطَ ٱلَّذِينَ أَنْعَمْتَ عَلَيْهِمْ ۝ غَيْرِ ٱلْمَغْضُوبِ عَلَيْهِمْ وَلَا ٱلضَّآلِّينَ ۝

بِسْمِ ٱللَّهِ ٱلرَّحْمَٰنِ ٱلرَّحِيمِ ۝

قُلْ أَعُوذُ بِرَبِّ ٱلنَّاسِ ۝ مَلِكِ ٱلنَّاسِ ۝ إِلَٰهِ ٱلنَّاسِ ۝ مِن شَرِّ ٱلْوَسْوَاسِ ٱلْخَنَّاسِ ۝ ٱلَّذِى يُوَسْوِسُ فِى صُدُورِ ٱلنَّاسِ ۝ مِنَ ٱلْجِنَّةِ وَٱلنَّاسِ ۝

بِسْمِ ٱللَّهِ ٱلرَّحْمَٰنِ ٱلرَّحِيمِ ۝

قُلْ أَعُوذُ بِرَبِّ ٱلْفَلَقِ ۝ مِن شَرِّ مَا خَلَقَ ۝ وَمِن شَرِّ غَاسِقٍ إِذَا وَقَبَ ۝ وَمِن شَرِّ ٱلنَّفَّٰثَٰتِ فِى ٱلْعُقَدِ ۝ وَمِن شَرِّ حَاسِدٍ إِذَا حَسَدَ ۝

بِسْمِ ٱللَّهِ ٱلرَّحْمَٰنِ ٱلرَّحِيمِ

قُلْ هُوَ ٱللَّهُ أَحَدٌ ۝ ٱللَّهُ ٱلصَّمَدُ ۝ لَمْ يَلِدْ وَلَمْ يُولَدْ ۝ وَلَمْ يَكُن لَّهُۥ كُفُوًا أَحَدٌۢ ۝

   Completed on   /   /

▸▸ Read and memorise the Surahs.

Read one verse repeatedly to help memorise, then the next verse repeatedly. Join the two verses to test yourselves. Keep doing this until you learn the whole Surah.

- I can read the **Surahs from memory** fluently.
- I can implement all the lessons learnt previously into this exercise.

LESSON 45: LAST 10 SURAHS

بِسْمِ ٱللَّهِ ٱلرَّحْمَٰنِ ٱلرَّحِيمِ ۝

تَبَّتْ يَدَآ أَبِى لَهَبٍ وَتَبَّ ۝ مَآ أَغْنَىٰ عَنْهُ مَالُهُۥ وَمَا كَسَبَ ۝ سَيَصْلَىٰ نَارًا ذَاتَ لَهَبٍ ۝ وَٱمْرَأَتُهُۥ حَمَّالَةَ ٱلْحَطَبِ ۝ فِى جِيدِهَا حَبْلٌ مِّن مَّسَدٍۭ ۝

بِسْمِ ٱللَّهِ ٱلرَّحْمَٰنِ ٱلرَّحِيمِ ۝

إِذَا جَآءَ نَصْرُ ٱللَّهِ وَٱلْفَتْحُ ۝ وَرَأَيْتَ ٱلنَّاسَ يَدْخُلُونَ فِى دِينِ ٱللَّهِ أَفْوَاجًا ۝ فَسَبِّحْ بِحَمْدِ رَبِّكَ وَٱسْتَغْفِرْهُ ۚ إِنَّهُۥ كَانَ تَوَّابًۢا ۝

بِسْمِ ٱللَّهِ ٱلرَّحْمَٰنِ ٱلرَّحِيمِ ۝

قُلْ يَٰٓأَيُّهَا ٱلْكَٰفِرُونَ ۝ لَآ أَعْبُدُ مَا تَعْبُدُونَ ۝ وَلَآ أَنتُمْ عَٰبِدُونَ مَآ أَعْبُدُ ۝ وَلَآ أَنَا۠ عَابِدٌ مَّا عَبَدتُّمْ ۝ وَلَآ أَنتُمْ عَٰبِدُونَ مَآ أَعْبُدُ ۝ لَكُمْ دِينُكُمْ وَلِىَ دِينِ ۝

بِسْمِ ٱللَّهِ ٱلرَّحْمَٰنِ ٱلرَّحِيمِ ۝

إِنَّآ أَعْطَيْنَٰكَ ٱلْكَوْثَرَ ۝ فَصَلِّ لِرَبِّكَ وَٱنْحَرْ ۝ إِنَّ شَانِئَكَ هُوَ ٱلْأَبْتَرُ ۝

   Completed on   /   /

⁍ Read and memorise the Surahs.

Read one verse repeatedly to help memorise, then the next verse repeatedly. Join the two verses to test yourselves. Keep doing this until you learn the whole Surah.

- I can read the **Surahs from memory** fluently.
- I can implement all the lessons learnt previously into this exercise.

LESSON 45 — LAST 10 SURAHS

بِسْمِ ٱللَّهِ ٱلرَّحْمَٰنِ ٱلرَّحِيمِ

أَرَءَيْتَ ٱلَّذِى يُكَذِّبُ بِٱلدِّينِ ۝ فَذَٰلِكَ ٱلَّذِى يَدُعُّ ٱلْيَتِيمَ ۝ وَلَا يَحُضُّ عَلَىٰ طَعَامِ ٱلْمِسْكِينِ ۝ فَوَيْلٌ لِّلْمُصَلِّينَ ۝ ٱلَّذِينَ هُمْ عَن صَلَاتِهِمْ سَاهُونَ ۝ ٱلَّذِينَ هُمْ يُرَآءُونَ ۝ وَيَمْنَعُونَ ٱلْمَاعُونَ ۝

بِسْمِ ٱللَّهِ ٱلرَّحْمَٰنِ ٱلرَّحِيمِ ۝

لِإِيلَٰفِ قُرَيْشٍ ۝ إِۦلَٰفِهِمْ رِحْلَةَ ٱلشِّتَآءِ وَٱلصَّيْفِ ۝ فَلْيَعْبُدُوا۟ رَبَّ هَٰذَا ٱلْبَيْتِ ۝ ٱلَّذِىٓ أَطْعَمَهُم مِّن جُوعٍ ۝ وَءَامَنَهُم مِّنْ خَوْفٍۭ ۝

بِسْمِ ٱللَّهِ ٱلرَّحْمَٰنِ ٱلرَّحِيمِ ۝

أَلَمْ تَرَ كَيْفَ فَعَلَ رَبُّكَ بِأَصْحَٰبِ ٱلْفِيلِ ۝ أَلَمْ يَجْعَلْ كَيْدَهُمْ فِى تَضْلِيلٍ ۝ وَأَرْسَلَ عَلَيْهِمْ طَيْرًا أَبَابِيلَ ۝ تَرْمِيهِم بِحِجَارَةٍ مِّن سِجِّيلٍ ۝ فَجَعَلَهُمْ كَعَصْفٍ مَّأْكُولٍۭ ۝

Completed on   /   /

•➤ Read and memorise the Surahs.

Read one verse repeatedly to help memorise, then the next verse repeatedly. Join the two verses to test yourselves. Keep doing this until you learn the whole Surah.

- I can read the Surahs from memory fluently.
- I can implement all the lessons learnt previously into this exercise.

STUDENT CHECKLIST

- I am able to read the entire Alphabet from memory.
- I am able to recognise all letters in different forms.
- I am able to read and spell words that have Fat-hah above them.
- I am able to read and spell words that have Kasrah beneath them.
- I am able to read and spell words that have Dhammah above them.
- I am able to read and spell words that have Fat-ha-tayn above them.
- I am able to read and spell words that have Kasra-tayn beneath them.
- I am able to read and spell words that have Dhamma-tayn above them.
- I am able to read and spell words that have Fat-hah followed by an Alif.
- I am able to read and spell words that have Madd Fat-hah above them.
- I am able to read and spell words that have Madd Kasrah beneath them.
- I am able to read and spell words that have Madd Dhammah above them.
- I am able to read and spell words that have Sukoon on them.
- I am able to read and spell words that have Fat-hah followed by a Waw Saakin.
- I am able to read and spell words that have Dhammah followed by a Waw Saakin.
- I am able to read and spell words that have Fat-hah followed by a Ya Saakin.
- I am able to read and spell words that have Kasrah followed by a Ya Saakin.

STUDENT CHECKLIST

- I am able to read and spell silent letters in words.
- I am able to read and spell the words that include a silent Alif.
- I am able to read and spell the special words used in the Qur'aan.
- I am able to read and spell words with a jerking sound.
- I am able to read and spell words that have Shaddah above them.
- I am able to read and spell words that have a small Madd.
- I am able to read and spell words that have a big Madd.
- I am able to read and spell words that have a big Madd followed a Shaddah.
- I am able to apply Qalqalah.
- I am able to apply Ghunnah.
- I am able to apply Izhaar.
- I am able to read the letter Ra as a Full Mouth/Empty Mouth Letter.
- I am able to read the word Allaah with a Full Mouth/Empty Mouth.
- I am able to apply Idghaam.
- I am able to apply Ikhfaa.
- I am able to apply the Meem Saakin rules.
- I am able to apply Iqlaab.
- I am able to read and spell words with Noon Qutni.
- I am able to apply all the Waqf Rules .
- I am able to apply Saktah and Waqfah.
- Advance stopping and joining
- Haroof Al Muqatta'aat / Waqf (Stopping)
- Complete Verse fluency
- Memorisation of the last 10 Surahs

كُتِبَ هٰذا المُصْحَفُ الكريمُ، وضُبِطَ عَلى مَايَوَافِقُ رِوايَة حفصٍ بن سُلَيمَانَ بن المغِيرَة الأَسدىّ الكُوفِّ لِقِراءة عَاصم بن أَبِى النَّجُود الكوفِّ التَّابِعِّ عن أَبِى عبد الرَّحمن عبد الله ابن حبيب السُّلمِىّ عن عثمان بن عقَّان ، وعلِىّ بن أَبِى طَالبٍ وزيد بن ثَابت ، وَأُبَىّ ابن كعب عن النَّبِىّ صَلَّى اللَّهُ عليه وسلّم .

This Mushaf was written and compiled according to the Riwaayah of Hafs bin Sulayman, bin Al Mugheerah Al Asady Al Koofy, through the Qiraa'ah of 'Aasim bin Abdirrahman Abdillaah ibn Habeeb As sulamy, from Uthmaan bin 'Affaan, Ali bin Abi Taalib, Zaid bin Thaabit, Ubay ibn Ka'b (RA) and from Nabee (SAW).

This Madeenah script (Arabic font) used in Qaa'idah is believed to be the script from Al-Khaleefah Al-Raashid Uthmaan (RA) and has been used for centries in Makkah, Al-Madeenah, Iraq and Ash-Shaam.

Copyright of minimuallims publications.
All rights reserved. No part of this book may be reproduced in its current form without prior permission in writing from the minimuallims publications.

If you would like a copy of this book or would like to leave any feedback contact Shaykh Ubaid ur Rahman on info@minimuallims.com.